ENDORSEMENTS

What Others Are Saying

"One of the great things about this career ministry is that it incorporates evangelism, discipleship and care, helping people of all ages and stages, from students to seniors, at all socioeconomic levels and ethnicities. The seven-step process and curriculum [in Created for Good Works] helps turn messes into masterpieces, and workers into worshippers."

PASTOR DERWIN L. GRAY
Founding and Lead Pastor, Transformation Church, Indian Land, SC, Author of Limitless Life, Hero and High-Definition Leadership

"Read the first eight pages of this book and you'll develop a clear vision of the need for career ministry at your church. Then, in the chapters that follow, Brian will show you what goes into an effective career ministry and how to get one started at your church. An important book for pastors and church leaders!"

STEVE GRISSOM
Founder, Church Initiative: Divorce Care & Grief Share

"What a great resource for pastoral care and congregational development as well as for developing a congregational ministry to help people discover their calling from God! It is very pragmatic and spirit-led."

REV. PHIL TOM
Pastor, Eastchester Presbyterian Church, Bronx, NY

CREATED
— for —
GOOD WORKS

Why the Church should help people find
JOBS, CAREERS, AND GOD'S CALLING

Phil,
Blessings to you
m ofe God's
masterpieces

B

BRIAN RAY

foreword by Pastor Derwin L. Gray

Published by Crossroads Career® Services Inc.

ISBN 978-0-9898995-3-6

Scripture quotations marked NASB taken from the New American Standard Bible®, Copyright © 1960, 1962, 1963, 1968, 1971, 1972, 1973, 1975, 1977, 1995 by The Lockman Foundation. Used by permission. (www.Lockman.org)

All other Scripture quotations, unless otherwise indicated, are taken from either the Holy Bible, New International Version®, NIV®. Copyright ©1973, 1978, 1984, 2011 by Biblica, Inc.™ Used by permission of Zondervan. All rights reserved worldwide. www.zondervan.com The "NIV" and "New International Version" are trademarks registered in the United States Patent and Trademark Office by Biblica, Inc.™

Cover Design: Juliann Itter, Jumay Designs
Interior Art and Layout Design: Juliann Itter, Jumay Designs
Content Editor: Gus Sabestinas
Copy Editor: Chris McGinn

Trade distribution is provided by Send the Light Distribution. To purchase this book for trade distribution, go to www.stl-distribution.com.

Crossroads Career Services Inc.

Publisher's Cataloging-in-Publication data
Ray, Brian C.

Created for Good Works : Why the Church should help people find Jobs , Careers , and God's Calling /
Brian Ray ; foreword by Pastor Derwin L. Gray.
pages cm
ISBN 978-0-9898995-3-6 (pbk.)
ISBN 978-0-9898995-4-3 (ebook)

1. Mission of the church. 2. Christianity --United States. 3. Vocational guidance. 4. Career development. 5. Work --Religious aspects --Christianity. I. Gray, Derwin L. II. Title.

HF5382.75 R39 2015   2015948124
650.1/4 –dc23

Printed in the USA

15 16 17 18 19 20 – 10 9 8 7 6 5 4 3 2 1
1st Printing

CONTENTS

For we are His workmanship, created in Christ Jesus for good works, which
God prepared beforehand so that we would walk in them.
Ephesians 2:10, NASB

FOREWORD

A year after we started Transformation Church, one of our families asked for help to pay an overdue utility bill. The husband was unemployed and discouraged.

Another member of our congregation was in the meeting, and he offered to help him get work. Three things happened. We paid the bill. A career ministry began. The husband got a fulltime job and more of Jesus in his life.

Today our career ministry (led by non-paid servant leaders) provides a weekly support group, quarterly workshops, and one-to-one coaching. The team just launched a four-week course for high school students and their parents. We are partnering with a state prison to develop and train men in a faith-based, Christ-centered, job readiness program.

One of the great things about this career ministry is that it incorporates evangelism, discipleship, and care, helping people of all ages and stages, from students to seniors, at all socioeconomic levels and ethnicities.

Most importantly, the seven-step process and curriculum is based on the truth of God's word by the enabling work of the Holy Spirit. It turns messes into masterpieces and workers into worshippers.

The servant leader in that first meeting is my friend and brother in Christ, Brian Ray, who wrote the Work Book on finding jobs, careers, and God's calling. He not only equipped and trained our career ministry team, but he coached me, my wife and our daughter on college exploration. He has also resourced and supported over 100 other churches across the country.

As a fellow pastor and church leader, I invite you to read through this book. Consider your congregation and community in light of them all being created for good works, but they don't know it, yet.

Founding and Lead Pastor Derwin L. Gray
TRANSFORMATION CHURCH, INDIAN LAND, SC

Author of "Limitless Life, Hero and The High-Definition Leader: Building Multiethnic Churches in a Multiethnic World."

INTRODUCTION

Where does the Church fit in? How can we help those in need? We see the need every day, but figuring out what to do about it can be an overwhelming prospect.

Meet Julie. She is one of over 150 million people in the American workforce, and she can't stand going to work each day. Like Julie, over 50% of people who are employed are dissatisfied with their jobs.

Meet Bill. He has been actively looking for a job like 20 million others who are unemployed or underemployed.

Meet Tom. He loves his job, and he's great at it! But he wants his life to be more purposeful. Tom wants to make a difference with the skills he has.

Everyone desires fruitful and fulfilling work, but most have no idea that God created them for good works. How about you? Maybe you are a pastor or leader in a church. If so, you probably do understand that you are God's creation commissioned to walk in works God prepared for you. However, are you experiencing it every day? Are you clear about how God has made you? Can you discern which works are the ones He arranged for you?

Perhaps you lead or work for a parachurch organization, missions agency, Christian school, or community ministry. Possibly you are paid and on staff or you are volunteering. You might even be an individual who has gone through his or her own career transition or life transformation and wants to help others.

Whatever experience and role you have, do you feel trained and equipped to help others realize that they are masterpieces made for good works not only at work, but also in their whole lives? Can you help people see the good works God has prepared for them? Can you bridge the highly felt needs people have for profitable and meaningful work to the real needs of their heart and soul for Jesus Christ? Consider the ministry connection between these two facts.

1. *The number one thing that most people want is a good job, according to the Gallup® World Poll.*[1]

2. *The number one Person everyone needs is Jesus.*

MISSING MINISTRY FOUND

There is a global epidemic affecting every person, economy, and country on the planet. It is an allergic reaction caused by sin. Millions of people suffer and die every year from this dreaded disease. It causes unemployment, poverty, slavery, and war. Most people who have good jobs suffer from irritability, anxiety, dissatisfaction, and disengagement. Some are workaholics. Others are sloths. All need help, hope, and healing. Everyone needs a healer, including pastors and ministry leaders, as well as members of local churches and communities.

Jesus Is The Healer. His body, the Church, is to minister to its members and offer ministry to all. Yet, there is evidence that most pastors and churches are not equipped to evangelize, disciple, or care for people in their work lives. Even in the midst of the most recent economic and employment crisis, most churches were not even considering a ministry to help their congregations and communities.[2] In fact, many churches were cutting budgets, laying off staff, and closing their doors.[3]

The good news is that the missing ministry in most churches has been found. Over the past 15 years, the Crossroads Career Network ministry has served 446 churches and ministries. Pastors and ministry leaders are helping people hear and follow God's calling as it relates to work-life issues, career development, and even job search. Today we have in our network 82 churches and organizations offering faith-based, Christ-centered ministries to help people find jobs, careers, and God's calling. Our latest monthly newsletter emailing went to 33,000 subscribers from jobseekers and career explorers to pastors, ministry leaders, and teammates.

We are not only learning from our own network, but also from Christian workplace-focused leaders.

Tim Keller in his book *Every Good Endeavor* lays a strong foundation for faith and work together, proclaiming "Your daily work is ultimately an act of worship to the God who called and equipped you to do it – no matter what kind of work it is."[4] How blessed to work as worship. Imagine rejoicing in the midst of labor.

Amy Sherman in her book *Kingdom Calling* describes rejoicing as "dancing in the streets." She writes about vocational stewardship for the common good as "the intentional and strategic deployment of our vocational power – knowledge, platform, networks, position, influence, skills, and reputation – to advance foretastes of God's kingdom."[5] She goes on to say "If church leaders don't help parishioners discern how to live missionally through that work, they miss a major – in some instances **the** major – avenue believers have for learning to live as foretastes."[6]

As faith-at-work and marketplace ministries seek to bring Christ into people's lives Monday through Friday, they need an entry point where people are ready to listen, hear, and follow God. May I suggest that the tip of the arrow into people's work lives is helping them at decisive moments in their careers. It's called career ministry.

Because the number one thing that most people want is a good job, career ministry addresses a critical part of day-to-day living for three reasons.

1. *Jobs are the primary sources of our income and financial sustainability.*

2. *Work consumes an average of 45 hours/week of a person's life, about 40% of our waking hours.*

3. *People often find their personal identity and well-being in their careers.*

How often have you faced a situation in your ministry where a family is falling apart and the root problem seems to be financial instability? How many times a week does someone come into your church looking for food, shelter, or money to help with rent or utilities? The next time you hear—"Can you help me? I lost my job. I hate my job. I want God's calling"—you can have good answers to these questions, when you have a career ministry in your church. Career ministry can be a catalytic part of the "Big Three Ministries" in every local church...

EVANGELISM because people in the community come to the church for job and career issues—especially if they are unemployed.

DISCIPLESHIP because people in the church also have work issues, many times because they have an incomplete or incorrect view of work life being separate from their spiritual life.

CARE because job loss and work crises are often directly related to personal and individual counseling, financial ministries, and benevolence.

For example, financial ministries typically deal with debt and budgeting—the expense side of the ledger. Career ministry deals with the income side: how to do your current work better or find a different job that pays more.

Benevolence is another ministry in need of career ministry help. A family comes to the church to help get a utility bill paid or for food from the pantry. It's good to help fill these immediate needs, but career ministry can address the root problem: unemployment .

Your church has a critical mission in the community where God has placed you and at its core is the commission to reach people with the love of God. This book is designed to help you fulfill that mission by meeting people in the area of their most keenly felt needs. I'm not asking you to start a new program and add it to everything else that you're already doing. I'm asking you to allow God to open your eyes. It's more than likely that you'll discover this ministry already exists, at least in seed form, in your congregation, and that all the people, tools, and things you need for a successful career ministry are well within your reach. All they need is a platform and resources.

IN THE BEGINNING... WORK
In the beginning God created the heavens and the earth. Genesis 1:1

Then He made men and women in His image to be fruitful, multiply, fill the earth and subdue it, and rule over the animals.

God saw all He had done and said, "It was very good."

> By the seventh day God completed His work, which He had done, and He rested on the seventh day from all His work which He had done.
> Genesis 2:2, NASB

God worked, and He gave us work. He took man and put him in the Garden of Eden to cultivate and keep it with instructions that from any tree he could eat, except do not eat from tree of the knowledge of good and evil. He then created woman with the man, and the two became joined together in work and life as husband and wife.

The purpose of this book is to cast a vision, build a solid case, and call to action the Church to offer career ministry, because...

> We are His workmanship,
> created in Christ Jesus for good works,
> which God prepared beforehand that we would walk in them.
> Ephesians 2:10, NASB

I first saw the opportunity for this ministry when I joined the Chick-fil-A restaurant chain. I was responsible for human resources, operator ventures, and administration at a time when the corporate purpose had just been established: "To glorify God by being a faithful steward of all that is entrusted to us and to have a positive influence on all who come into contact with Chick-fil-A."

Part of my job was recruiting store operators and filling positions at the home office. Over 10,000 people per year were inquiring for less than a hundred openings. I wondered what happened to the 9,900 who were turned away every year? Perhaps there was a way we could have a positive influence. We developed processes to appreciate and encourage everyone we touched, even though we had to say "no" at the time.

After I left Chick-fil-A and started my executive search business, I invited candidates to career group meetings. Early Monday mornings we met at the office, not only for everyone to share career guidance and job search tips, but also to pray for and encourage one another.

By 1997 we had more people than space. Since my church had empty rooms during some of the weekdays and nights, I asked if there was a place we could meet. During the church leadership meeting, I asked what turned out to be a critically important question: "Since we are receiving support and doing ministry in the church, may we put ourselves under your authority?"

They looked at each other—seemingly not sure what to say. I told them that as a group accountable to God for their church, they had wisdom and prayer power. "Yes!" they said. I reported to an associate pastor, and we were accountable to the church.

God's ministering through us actually became a ministry of the church. Each meeting was an adventure with God. Who would He bring? What would they need? How could we help?

After a Saturday conference with 453 guests hearing speakers and attending workshops, two men walked the center aisle of the empty sanctuary toward me. One man was tall, well dressed, and crying. The other was a friend volunteering at the event, and he looked concerned. He said to me, "I just met John on the front steps, and he had questions. I told him about Jesus, and he accepted Christ. What do we do now?" What a perfect place for that question!

I can still see the scene in my mind. What a priceless moment engraved in my brain, to witness an out-of-work executive meet Jesus and enter into the Kingdom.

ON YOUR MARK, GET SET, GO!

Let us run with endurance the race that is set before us, fixing our eyes on Jesus. Hebrews 12:1-2, NASB

This book is organized into three main parts:

PART 1: ON YOUR MARK explains the target and the vision for career ministry – "the why" of it. Our starting point is to understand God's heart for people and how career issues influence people's walk of faith so we can effectively minister through this area of their lives.

PART 2: GET SET presents "the what" of career ministry, which is the 7-step process we use in ministering to people through the Crossroads Career Network. This section will give you a basic understanding of the concepts of Christ-centered career ministry so you can help people find jobs, careers, and God's calling.

PART 3: GO is all about "the how" to equip your church or organization to start and grow your own career ministry. This section will give you the tools to identify leaders, build a team, and help people follow God's calling and strengthen the Church.

PART 1

On Your Mark

FIVE HIGHEST FELT NEEDS

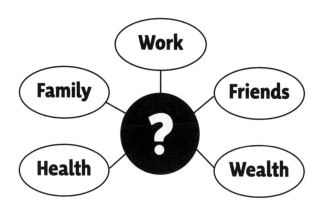

THE ONE REAL NEED

CHAPTER 1

The #1 Thing
MOST PEOPLE WANT

The largest behavioral economic research company on the planet, Gallup, Inc., created the World Poll that represents what seven million people think in nearly every country and every demographic and socio-graphic group imaginable. The chairman of Gallup, Jim Clifton, reported:

> **"Six years into our global data collection effort, we may have already found the single most searing, clarifying, helpful, world-altering fact.**
>
> **What the whole world wants is a good job. This is one of the most important discoveries Gallup has ever made."** [1]

If the number one thing most people want is a good job, then what are the implications of this highly felt need in ministering to their real spiritual needs?

How does unemployment, underemployment, misemployment, and even happy employment relate to the church's core ministries of evangelism, discipleship, and care? Does helping people with their jobs, careers, and God's calling link to their salvation, sanctification, and service?

I LOST MY JOB!
When someone you know or a member of your church asks for help because they lost their job, what thoughts come to your mind? How do you feel? Do you have a good answer? What can you do to help?

At the height of the employment crisis, *Christianity Today* reported:

> **"A February 2009 LifeWay Research survey of 1,000 Protestant churches nationwide found that 31% were considering creating or expanding ministries for the unemployed. Sixty-two percent had been approached for help by persons from their community, while 31% had been approached by their own church members."** [2]

When just one person asks for help because of unemployment, it can be a big, multi-faceted, potentially life-threatening problem.

First of all, if you lose your job, paychecks quit coming. No work, no money, no eating, no clothing, no place to live. Financial insecurity leads to personal loss of identity and vulnerability. Health is endangered by illness, accident, or assault. Wounds and sickness might go without care.

Second, job loss threatens marriage and family. Spouses can become anxious and angry. With the average period of unemployment exceeding six months, husbands and wives wonder what is the matter that another job is so hard to find. As I am writing these words, I am helping the spouses of two different marriages that blew up because one of the spouses in each was laid-off and had trouble finding the next job.

Third, it is tough to keep friends. You can't go do stuff with them, because most things cost money. Going to dinner. Seeing movies. Golf. After a while, they don't want to have to pick up the tab again. They wonder what's wrong. They are not sure what to say, so they say nothing. They don't call, email, or text. It's tough to make new friends, especially when most conversations start with, "So what do you do for a living?"

Fourth, being alone turns to feeling lonely. Emotions range from embarrassment to shame. Feelings of hurt, fear, and anger take turns beating you down. Self-respect leaves. Depression follows. Professional counseling is often needed but cannot be afforded.

God created us for good works. Even in the perfect place with everything provided, man had to keep and cultivate the Garden of Eden. If we are not working, then we must be sinning, right? Doesn't the Bible say that if a man will not work, do not let him eat?

Here is just one of millions of stories of distress. A 57-year-old software saleswoman in Seattle lost her job. After three years of looking and not finding a job, the solution she sought was swallowing a bunch of pills.[3]

"There was a reason: I had no hope. There was no point for the future. I had just lost another job opportunity that I thought I had done a really good job at, and they just dismissed me. I was old, and they're not going to hire me. With that, I couldn't have my life back."

She did not remember calling 911, but she did. Now she is managing more successfully since connecting with a local church and finding part-time work. "The fact that I've been able to get some temp jobs makes me feel like I am still worth something."

While she survived, others have not. With both the Great Depression in the 1930s and the more recent Great Recession starting in 2007, suicide rates spiked with the downturn of the economy and employment, according to studies by the Centers for Disease Control and Prevention and Suicide Prevention Resource Center.[4]

A couple of years ago, a prayer request with the keyword "suicide" was flagged on our website. We were able to find the long-term unemployed man and connect him to a local church and a government-funded career center.

I HATE MY JOB!

Most people are dissatisfied with their jobs. In 2013, the percentage of workers satisfied with their jobs was only 47.7%, according to The Conference Board's annual survey of job satisfaction.[5]

The Gallup 2013 survey report of Employee Engagement shows that 7 in 10 American workers are "not engaged" or "actively disengaged" in their work, meaning they are emotionally disconnected from their workplaces and less likely to be productive.[6]

While unemployment is most urgent and critical, those who are misemployed are more plentiful and pouting, because 50 to 75% of everyone who works is either dissatisfied or unengaged or both. Symptoms range from showing up for work just for the paycheck to being rebellious.

Since more of our waking hours are spent working than any other single activity, **misemployment can destroy attitudes and undermine aptitudes.** Here are some of the more common indicators you may be experiencing if you're disengaged at work:

- *Stress*
- *Dislike the work*
- *Working for a bad boss*
- *Not very good at the job*
- *Spending too many hours*
- *Not making enough money*
- *Worried about being laid-off*
- *Bored in a rut or a dead-end job*
- *Feeling used, abused, and refused*
- *Do not believe in the organization's culture, products, or services*
- *Want to be "on your own" as a contractor or maybe own a business*
- *Spending too much time "on the road again" traveling or commuting*
- *All of the above*

In the 1950s, popular singer Tennessee Ernie Ford recorded "Sixteen Tons" about a coal miner's toil and trouble. It quickly sold over a million copies. Perhaps the lyrics would still resonate with millions of people today.

> "You load 16 tons, and what do you get?
> Another day older and deeper in debt.
> Saint Peter don't call me 'cause I can't go.
> I owe my soul to the company store."

Pastors and ministry leaders are largely unaware of the negative impact of being miserably employed, because, as Henry David Thoreau described in his book, *Walden*:

> "The mass of men lead lives of quiet desperation. What is called resignation is confirmed desperation."

The same is true for most women, and that's important for two reasons.

1. *Nearly 60% of women are employed.* [6]

2. *Women make up more than 40% of the American workforce.* [7]

So, in summary, misemployment is a bigger problem than anyone imagines, which means it is an equally great opportunity for ministry.

I WANT GOD'S CALLING!

For most of my career, I have worked with successfully employed executives. Many of them loved their jobs, but they found that earning another dollar was neither motivating nor satisfying. They were looking for meaning, purpose, or significance. Some retired and started giving back, but even the philanthropy of time, talent, and treasure left them empty.

One of my clients was president of an insurance company and owner of a football team. He had more of what seemed like everything than anybody I know. Yet, I rarely saw him smile. He was always reaching for more and was never satisfied.

Even one of the most successful men in the history of the world had his issues with work. As the author of Ecclesiastes, he summed up his feelings of futility this way...

> Vanity of vanities! All is vanity. What advantage does man have in all his work which he does under the sun? Ecclesiastes 1:2-3, NASB

It is not until you submit all of who you are, what you do, and what you possess to the Lord that you can receive the hope of His calling, the riches of His glory, and the greatness of His power. Then, and only then, can you delight yourself in the Lord and receive the desires of your heart. Then you can realize that you are employed for life, whether you love, hate, or lost your job.

THE LORD IS MY EMPLOYER

After 20 years of working with small groups of Christian job-seekers, my friend Barbara Rarden has written a great perspective in her book *Employed for Life*.

> "The Lord is my Employer.
> I shall never be out of work.
> He makes me to be His representative.
> He leads me to places where I can be a blessing."[8]

All of a sudden this point of view redefines employment. God made us to work for Him, as He works in and through us. With God as our Employer, we are always employed, regardless of whether we are unemployed, underemployed, misemployed, or happily employed.

Being employed for life has two meanings for me...

1. *I am employed by God all of my life.*

2. *God's employment is my life.*

God's word and Gallup research seem to agree that work is simply about what we do every day, whether we are students, employees, employers, homemakers, or retirees. If we are breathing and reasonably healthy, we are to be occupied with work in some form or fashion.

If God is our Employer and we are employed for life, then we have to take another look at employment statistics. Instead of focusing only on the 150 million plus Americans in the workforce, we should look at our total population of over 300 million. Maybe it is even better to consider shifting our focus globally from a workforce of 3 billion to our entire planet's population of 7.3 billion people. Or perhaps it is more helpful to look at the local workforce and population statistics of your own county, knowing that **each person was created on purpose and for a purpose.** Whether local or global, what a high calling to help people realize that they are God's workmanship created for good works prepared for them.

EARTHLY GOOD

Jesus connected with people and their felt needs. He started with where people were, and then He brought them to where He wanted them to be. In other words, He was relevant to the needs that people felt.

Have you ever heard the phrase "So heavenly minded, you're no earthly good?" Did you know it was in a song by Johnny Cash? Let me give you a few lines.

Come heed me, my brothers, come heed, one and all.
Don't brag about standing or you'll surely fall.
You're shining your light and shine it you should.
But you're so heavenly minded, you're no earthly good.
If you're holding heaven, then spread it around.
There's hungry hands reaching up here from the ground.[9]

It is easy to be so taken with the glory of God that we forget many people are daily struggling at work and at home and in between. It's easy to get so focused on Sunday that faith seems to be irrelevant Monday through Friday. If you sat down with most church leaders today and asked them about the biggest challenges they face, they will probably mention disengaged members somewhere near the top of the list. Apathy spreads like a virus through the American church, and it's difficult to stamp out. Could the root of this epidemic have something to do with the disconnect between Sunday and Monday? Is it possible that members *want* to be more engaged, but just don't see the relevance from what's taught in the pulpit to what they do from nine-to-five each weekday?

Researcher George Barna in his book *Growing True Disciples* reported "**eight out of every ten believers are more likely to count dimensions of life other than spirituality as the springboard to success and meaning.** Elements such as family, career development, and financial achievement are among the emphases most likely to divert people's attention from their spiritual growth."[10] To reach and minister to people, it is critical to know their felt needs and how they think about them.

Imagine a family walking into your church for a Sunday service for the first time. They've put on their best clothes, so they look nice on the outside, but inside they're desperate. It's been seven months without income from a job, and it's become a struggle to put food on the table and pay the rent. They haven't come because they know their need for salvation. They have come because they know their need for hope. What will they see, what will they hear at your church? Will it give them hope for their future? People come hungry for hope ... are we feeding them?

JESUS KNOWS WHERE THE FISH ARE

Seven men had spent all night fishing. It was early morning, and they had caught nothing. All of them were uncertain about their future. They had been part of something great together, but now they weren't sure if that particular line of work was going to continue. A few of them had been professional fisherman before, so it added insult to injury that they couldn't seem to net one fish.

And then some stranger starts yelling at them from the shore, telling them to cast their net on the other side of the boat. Can you imagine how astonished Jesus' disciples were when they cast their net and felt the boat lurch? The haul of fish was nothing short of miraculous. For Peter, it was reminiscent of how Jesus first called him away from his occupation as a fisherman and into his calling, so he threw himself overboard and swam to shore. The rest paddled and struggled with the boat and the net. How tired and hungry everyone was. Arriving on shore, they discovered Jesus had already made a fire and was cooking.

I love the way Jesus teaches. After three years of discipleship, He is now getting His men ready to launch the ministry He is giving them. It is like the last lesson before He leaves the planet, and they graduate to conquer the world. He knew their immediate need for food and rest, so He prepared everything and invited them to eat. I imagine everyone had seconds. They are full and feeling their fatigue. What a perfect time for the punch line.

FEED MY SHEEP

Jesus said to Simon Peter, "Simon son of John, do you love me more than these?" "Yes, Lord," he said, "you know that I love you." Jesus said, "Feed my lambs." Again Jesus said, "Simon son of John, do you love me?" He answered, "Yes, Lord, you know that I love you." Jesus said, "Take care of my sheep." The third time he said to him, "Simon son of John, do you love me?" Peter was hurt because Jesus asked him the third time, "Do you love me?" He said, "Lord, you know all things; you know that I love you." Jesus said, "Feed my sheep." John 21: 15-17, NASB

In asking these questions and giving these commands, **Jesus was meeting a greater need in Peter than his hunger for fish and bread.** Peter needed a purpose, and that purpose was to feed God's people. Jesus knows where the fish are. He knows how to give us what we need, when we need it. He knows how to meet our felt needs in order to bring us to a place where we understand our true need to follow Him.

Jesus was giving Peter a new perspective on his career and calling. Peter was ready to go back to his old career in fishing, but Jesus was telling him it's time to be a shepherd. Career ministry isn't just for the jobless and disgruntled individuals who walk through the doors of our churches. It's for all of us—sheep and shepherds alike. Everyone needs career ministry.

CHAPTER 2

The #1 Person
EVERYONE NEEDS

ONLY JESUS

Everyone I know goes through tough times. For some, it is loss. For others, hurt. For many, it is being used, abused, and refused. For me, it was two years of all that and more.

In 1990, my wife left. My son went to jail. My business went to zero. The house was sold. Savings and retirement evaporated. Most of my friends abandoned me. I felt unwelcome at church.

I moved into my rented office and slept on a borrowed couch. I showered and dressed at a local gym. The main meal of the day was a Whopper®.

It was just me and Jesus. That is when I discovered the reality that when Jesus was all I had, Jesus was all I needed.

I had accepted Christ 19 years earlier and grew in my faith by His word and prayer in fellowship with others. But this trial was like nothing I had ever experienced. It took me three years to dig out from under the rubble, as the Lord lifted me one day at a time. Before God could build me up, He broke me down.

It hurt. It was awful. It was wonderful. The suffering was purifying. In the midst of it all, only Jesus in me, the hope of glory, was saying:

> The thief comes only to steal and kill and destroy; I came that they may have life, and have it abundantly. John 10:10, NASB

Yes, in the midst of it all, Jesus calls it abundant life. Jeremiah refers to it as a future and a hope. My pastor, Derwin Gray, calls it love in three ways. Loving God completely (Upward). Loving ourselves correctly (Inward). Loving our neighbors compassionately (Outward).[1]

I like the flow of his thinking because it comes from above, in, and through me to everyone else. It speaks to all three of my lives as a human being – body, soul, and spirit.

- **My Public Life** *is expressed outwardly through my body loving people compassionately, from spouse to family, friends to community, health to wealth, and work.*
- **My Personal Life** *is all about my soul — mind, will, and emotions. This is the place where I can love myself correctly as I think, feel, and make decisions.*
- **My Private Life:** *The core of who I am is spirit. The only Person in my private life is God the Father, Son, and Holy Spirit, being loved completely with all my heart, soul, and mind.*

In its simplest form, here is what we look like, body, soul, and spirit.

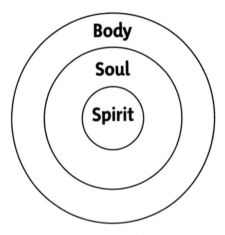

The problem is that most people start looking and loving inward and outward, before they look and love upward. They busy themselves with their own self-interests.

After 40 years of talking with more than 25,000 people about their jobs, careers, work, and life, I realized the need for a Christ-centered, whole-life perspective. Let's begin with the five highest felt needs that people face.

Family: Mom and dad, brothers and sisters, husband and wife, sons and daughters by blood and marriage both extended and blended.

Friends: Neighbors in communities of work, school, church, neighborhoods, ethnicity, citizenship, and commons interests both current and yet to be met.

Health: Feeling good and being well. Free from illness and pain. Physically fit and strong with energy and endurance.

Wealth: Being financially secure. Having money, property, possessions, and investments. Being rich, affluent, and prosperous.

Work: What you do every day. Whether you are a student, employee, employer, volunteer, or retired, it is the fruitful and fulfilling investment of your time and talents.

These five areas overlap and interact for better or worse. When one of these areas is set afire by crisis, other areas can get burned as well. Problems in the family can negatively impact your ability to work. Poor work performance can put your financial stability at risk. The stress of work and financial worries will hurt your health. Issues in your health, wealth, work, or family can make community with friends difficult.

Personal crises are points of pain and windows of opportunity for the Church, the body of Christ, to be the hands and feet of Jesus. If there is a severe work issue, many times those who are suffering are embarrassed or even ashamed. They hide behind fake smiles and "everything is fine" answers. Shepherds in the Church need to watch the flock, especially those who wander away or fall down. Be attentive and graceful to stay alert for one-line comments of despair or anxiety that beg for a follow-up question. Be prepared with equipped and trained ministry team members who have a platform and process for helping – quietly and confidentially.

Examples abound.

My friend Jim called me one day very upset. His wife left him for another guy. Oh, how he was hurt. Try as he might, his work performance started to slip. After a few weeks, his boss came to him and sympathized with Jim's depression. He told Jim he understood how hard this was, but it was impacting his performance, so he let Jim go. Immediately Jim had two new problems—no job and no income. His sudden financial misfortune threatened his ability to keep the big house he had bought for him and his wife. He had to sell it as fast as he could to get out from under the payments, but he had to take less than the house was worth. Of course that further impacted his chances of getting his wife back. Jim's health started to slip—over-eating, under-exercising, depressed.

Jim is not alone. According to a recent Gallup survey...

"The longer that Americans are unemployed, the more likely they are to re-port signs of poor psychological well-being. About one in five Americans who have been unemployed for a year or more say they currently have or are being treated for depression—almost double the rate among those who have been unemployed for five weeks or less. Programs geared toward helping American job seekers maintain psychological, physical, and social aspects of well-being over the course of their job search may help them to re-enter the workforce ready to be as productive as they were when they left."[2]

Jim reached out for help. His friends started to drift away. They weren't really sure what to say about all the bad things happening, so they said nothing. They just did not call. A handful of us came to his rescue—all of us brothers in the faith: a real estate broker, a financial planning professional, a good friend, and me to help with the career part. It was the Church in action.

The reverse is also true. A positive move in any one or combination of your felt needs can positively influence the other areas. I heartily recommend daily time with Jesus and weekly check-ups in all five areas of felt needs.

BALANCING ACT

Sometimes life feels like a circus, and you are the act on the high wire. To fully live the abundant life, somehow you have to achieve balance by centering.

Just ask Nikolas "Nik" Wallenda, famous acrobat, aerialist, daredevil, high wire artist, and holder of nine Guinness World Records. Perhaps you were one of 23 million people in the U.S. who watched him live on the Discovery channel in 2013 when he became the first person to cross the Grand Canyon on a wire, un-tethered, 1,500 feet above the Little Colorado River, with wind gusts measured up to 48 miles per hour.

In his book *Balance: A Story of Faith, Family, and Life on the Line*, Nik begins as follows...

"God is my center. God's grace is the balancing pole that keeps me from fall-ing into self-obsession and self-deceptions. Whatever I have achieved—and will ever achieve—is the result of my relationship with Him."[3]

More than a billion TV viewers watched as Nik walked across the roaring Ni-agara, praying aloud every step of the way. Then he returned the next day and spent more than three hours picking up trash left by the crowds to keep fame and glory at bay. Balance is about centering.

The biomechanics of acrobats are maintaining balance by positioning their center of mass directly over their base of support. The most critical part is the stability and reliability of your base of support.

Abundant life requires **centering your whole being in God the Father, His Son Jesus Christ, and the Holy Spirit as your base of support**. Your spirit and soul—your mind, will, and emotions—abide in Christ, and you're changed from glory to glory. Everything else in your life—all that you hold dear—is brought into alignment with the One True God.

HOME AND WORK

It is also important to see how the five felt-need phases of our lives interact, and then to submit them to the Lordship of Christ.

We've all heard the phrase, "Don't bring work home." It's easier said than done.

My friend Todd, a VP in a multi-billion dollar financial firm, got shuffled into a new job with a new boss. The job is not in his sweet spot, and he does not have the knowledge and skills to do it. The boss is providing no orientation or training, but is nitpicking the results. As Todd is making progress, his boss takes the improvements, shares no compliments, and takes credit for himself. I don't know about you, but I am already mad. Imagine how Todd feels. If he retaliates, he could be fired. So Todd does his best and keeps his frustration until he gets home. The negative impact on Todd's wife and daughter is immediate and hurtful.

The good news for my friend Jennifer, a director in a healthcare company, is she makes four times the average wage earner in America. The bad news is that she is working 70 hours a week, and it's affecting her health. So, she can choose to take a sabbatical, which she cannot afford, or she can keep working and get sicker. The choice then is either wealth or health, but not both.

Listening to Delores talk about her son was very heartening. As a single parent, she worked two and sometime three jobs to pay the way for her family. It was tough on mother and son. But she believes that God has picked him for missions, and he believes it, too. Somehow, Jesus will see them through.

Bill hates going to work, especially when the sales team goes on the road. The work itself is wonderful, and Bill is great at it. It's after hours that's tough, when everybody else is headed out to eat, drink, and be merry. It is a lifestyle that does not fit his life values. The problem comes at promotion time. The boss knows the guys he has been partying with, but Bill—not so much. So, guess who gets the nod for the next step up?

The interplay of your work life and the rest of your life is no small thing. **Your job rules the rest because it fuels the rest.** For most of us, our primary source of wealth and financial security is a job.

The interplay of felt needs—essential elements of wellbeing in our lives—are tightly linked. Usually one or two of these elements dominate our lives for a period of time. For young single adults, friends and work may dominate the day-to-day. When older, health becomes a major theme. During your 30s through your 50s, major themes are likely to be family, work, and wealth.

Anyone can see the positive and negative effects of blood and marital relationships, especially spouses, children, and parents. Even issues far in the past regarding your family can significantly disrupt your feelings and activities with friends, in our health, wealth, and work.

When it comes to health, nothing takes down all other elements faster than a critical accident or illness. It can interrupt your work, wipe out your wealth, and overburden family and friends.

Work can be very impactful on your life. Disruption in someone's career can completely destroy financial wellbeing and family relationships. The emotional hit to a personal sense of self-worth can also hurt physical health and friend support.

Only one thing can lift up any one or all five elements of wellbeing—personal faith. This is why career ministry can become a major key in helping churches accomplish their key missions of evangelism, discipleship, and care. **A crisis at work can trigger not just career transition, but more importantly, life transformation.**

EVANGELISM

The Church spends countless hours and millions of dollars every year trying to find more effective ways to reach the lost. We employ all the same tools used by businesses and corporations to get the message out: websites, banner ads, email blasts, social media, mass mailers, billboards, television ads... These are all worthwhile endeavors, because the cause is worthy. If the Good Shepherd is so distracted by the lost sheep that he'd leave the ninety-nine to go after the one, then we ought to be using every tool available to find lost sheep, too.

The problem we run into is this: Jesus isn't a product to be sold or a commodity to be traded. He is all-or-nothing in our lives. He wants us hot or cold—there's no in-between. He ministers to the whole person, and He asks for us to be wholly devoted in return. The Church can certainly try to sell Jesus, but Jesus wasn't ever much of salesman Himself, at least not by worldly standards. His sales pitch was something like this: "You want to follow me? Okay, here's your cross—it's kinda heavy. There's going to be trials and persecution, and daily you'll deny yourself for my sake. You will most likely end up being martyred for me. But I will always be more than enough for you."

Boy, don't sugarcoat it for me, Jesus. Abundant life doesn't need to be sugarcoated, because it's not some pie-in-the-sky fantasy version of life. It's real life with all its warts, conflicts, and setbacks. But Jesus cares about the conflicts and setbacks. He cared about the withered hands, the issues of blood, and the blind eyes ... and He healed them. He cared about the hungry, and He fed them. And He cares about every one of our felt needs today. It's almost unfathomable that He takes time out of His busy schedule of keeping the stars spinning through the cosmos to love and care for me and my needs, but He does.

Is money important to God? God doesn't need money—He owns everything! But He's a good Father, and He knows that without money, I can't eat, I can't clothe myself, I can't provide for my family... And so money is important to Him, because it's important to me.

This message—that God cares for our needs—isn't something that should just be preached from the pulpit, it should be built into the structure of how we do church.

God is interested in every felt need: family, friends, health, wealth, and work. Most churches have structures and ministries addressing family needs—parenting classes, marriage counseling, etc. This is a good thing! We need strong families and strong marriages. Most churches also work hard to foster strong friendships through small groups, special-interest ministries, and the like. But how is your church or ministry doing when it comes to addressing the highest felt need of a good job?

Our challenge as the body of Christ is to build structures into our local churches that address these felt needs so that people don't fall through the cracks. When people come through the doors of your church or into your ministry and hear that God is interested in their career, you have their attention. When they further see that you have established tools and have a team of people ready to talk to them about their career, you've begun to win their heart. Yes, there are deeper needs of the soul, but most of us are blind to those needs until someone helps us address the most immediately felt need of having some sort of income. More often than not, the two needs are deeply intertwined, and ministering to the one helps open the door to addressing the other.

DISCIPLESHIP

Go and make disciples of all nations, baptizing them in the name of the
Father and of the Son and of the Holy Spirit, and teaching them to obey
everything I have commanded you. And surely I am with you always, to the
very end of the age. Matthew 28:19-20

For the longest time I could not get my head around the first word of this verse:
"Go!" My questions were, "Go where? When would I get the time? How? Where
am I going to get the money? I have a full time job. I am not free to travel. I don't
speak a foreign language."

Then I thought that going is not really for me, it's for missionaries—those people who are called to other nations in Africa or Asia are to go but not me. Maybe
my calling is to send others by making donations or praying. That could, sort
of, be my way to go.

I don't remember if a pastor said it, or in Bible study I read it, but **the word "go"
in the Great Commission, is actually better translated "as you are going."** My
whole perspective about my role in making disciples suddenly turned inside
out.

Wherever I am, I have the commission to make disciples. Not just if I go to China
or South Africa, but also when I go to church, home, or work. In fact, maybe
work more than the rest because of all the places I spend time, most of it is at
work somewhere—whether by phone, Internet, or in person. Any time is a
good time to make disciples—whether the opportunity is evangelism, discipleship, care, or something else. No special travel arrangements or fundraising are
required. I just need to be alert wherever I go and whatever I am doing.

Career ministry helps build disciples because it's about so much more than just
getting a job. It's about discovering God's calling for your life and pursuing it not
only on Sunday, but Monday through Saturday, too.

CARE

Why do family and friends, let alone fellow church members, sometimes feel
helpless about how to help someone who is unemployed? To be unemployed
is to be terribly on your own and incredibly lonely.

Creating and providing community for those who are alone is in some way providing pastoral care for everyone. It also serves as pre-evangelism to those who
find themselves unemployed and looking for support.

The community needs to reach out to those who are unemployed. In my experiences with people who have lost their jobs, I have learned about their loneliness and their feeling like outcasts. They may be keeping their situation quiet so that no one knows, because they're ashamed of what's happened to them.

Career ministry creates a safe place for those facing the stigma of joblessness. It also creates a hand up for those who had previously only received a handout. Whether your church has a benevolence ministry or not, you've probably seen many in need come through your doors asking for food or gas money, help with the electric bill, bus fare ... You've probably even seen the same individuals return multiple times with the same need. Caring for their immediate need can lead to caring for their greater need for a job, which can lead to their greatest need of hearing God's calling in their life.

Faith-based, Christ-centered living means you can master the now and the future. Submit to the Master, and He gives you the vision, wisdom, and power to take courage and master your days, moment by moment. For me, if I fix my eyes on Jesus every step of the way during every single day, then I stay focused and balanced.

The abundant life isn't for a select few. It's not for the elite. Jesus invited all to put their whole trust in him and to live to the fullest. We, as the Church, get to partner with Him in that call, and career ministry is an incredible tool to help us do it. Now let's focus in the next chapter on most people's highest felt need: Work!

REFLECTION QUESTIONS

1. *How would I collectively rank the five highest felt needs in my life? Why do I think that? What about others in my local church?*

2. *What does the Bible say about how to holistically balance the five high-felt needs related to work?*

3. *What is one spiritual next step from this chapter that I can share with my church or group? What is one practical next step?*

CHAPTER 3

The Church
AT WORK

By the Church, I don't mean church buildings or denominations, but rather all believers who are members of the body of Christ. I love the way the Apostle Paul described the Church at work.

> ...we are to grow up in all aspects into Him who is the head, even Christ, from whom the whole body, being fitted and held together by what every joint supplies, according to the proper working of each individual part, causes the growth of the body for the building up of itself in love.
> Ephesians 4:15-16, NASB

So, as a member of Christ's body, imagine getting up every day with the conviction that you are on the planet for a purpose. How fulfilled and fruitful would you be to know that you and your work matter to God and that He is pleased? How great would it be to experience real success?

What do I mean by real success? I mean a comprehensive success that transcends the workplace, a success that permeates your home, school, community, and all areas of your life. This success is not a fake that promises fulfillment and delivers only emptiness after you arrive.

Real success is accomplishing genuinely purposeful work, not only for blessings and benefits in this world, but also for eternal impact and rewards. Let's start by looking more closely at the four core parts of success in Ephesians 2:10...

> We are His workmanship
> Created in Christ Jesus for good works
> Which God prepared beforehand
> So that we would walk in them

If this is true, what are the implications and applications in your life, your work, and your relationships? Who are you as God's workmanship? What does it mean to be created in Christ Jesus for good works? How can you discover works God has already prepared? How will you walk in them? The answers to these questions lie in the truth that you can hear God's call—not only calling you into relationship, but also calling you to follow Him. This truth can transform success from a potential to a reality in you.

No matter what you are doing, you have the opportunity to define your existence by who you are—not just by what you do. Gary O'Malley, author of *Life Purpose in a Nutshell*, explains it this way:

> "If what you do is who you are,
> then when you don't, you aren't."[1]

Let's explore how you are gifted and impassioned. You are a one-of-a-kind creation.

Let me share with you a story about a meeting I wanted to have with a vice president of sales who had a reputation of being impossible to meet. To get his attention, and an appointment, I rented a homing pigeon. Seriously! I put a pigeon in a special delivery cage with the attached note:

> Introducing Flash, the homing pigeon.
> If you would like your sales to fly,
> please write a date and time that I can see you.
> Put your note in Flash's special pouch and let him go.

I included my business card and instructions. A few hours later, the pigeon's owner called. The pigeon had returned and I had an appointment with "Mr. Impossible."

There are two lessons that I took from this experience... First, there are people gifted and passionate about breeding, raising, and training homing pigeons. (There are others who are crazy enough to rent pigeons to get appointments.) Second, God intends for us to use our gifts—whatever they are—in service to others. When you do, you will likely be led to new and greater opportunities for service—not only at work, but also in every area of your life.

WHY WORK?

Work is the physical and mental energy exerted to be productive in what God has called and equipped us to do. This requires a change in focus. Instead of viewing work as a means to an end, yearning for the day you can retire, Scripture teaches we should derive fulfillment from labor because it is part of what we were created to do. Therefore, there are six reasons why we should work according to Roger Gum, financial planner and author of *Financial Faithfulness*. [2]

1. *God intended man to work and be productive*

   Then the Lord God took the man and put him in the Garden of Eden to cultivate it and keep it. Genesis 2:15, NASB

2. *Work provides fulfillment, a way to use our God-given gifts and skills.*

   Whatever you do, do it heartily, as for the Lord rather than men, knowing that from the Lord you will receive the reward of the inheritance; It is the Lord Christ whom you serve. Colossians 3:23-24, NASB

3. *Work provides an opportunity to provide for our families.*

   But if anyone does not provide for his own, and especially for those of his household, he has denied the faith and is worse than an unbeliever. 1 Timothy 5:8, NASB

4. *Work provides an opportunity to provide for others.*

   At the present time your plenty will supply what they need, so that in turn their plenty will supply what you need. 2 Corinthians 8:14, NASB

5. *Work provides an environment to live out our Christian life and witness to others.*

   You are the light of the world... Let your light so shine before men, that they may see your good works and glorify to your Father who is in heaven. Matthew 5:14-16, NASB

6. *We are commanded to work, so that we are not an unnecessary burden to others.*

   For even when we were with you, we used to give you this order: if anyone is not willing to work, then he is not to eat either. 2 Thessalonians 3:10, NASB

WORK IS BLESSED

In the first chapter of the first book of the Bible, God works. He creates the heavens, the earth, and everything on the earth. He makes us in His image, and blesses us.

God saw all that he had made, and it was very good. Genesis 1:31

In chapter two God gets more specific about the work, commanding man to cultivate and keep the garden and to enjoy the fruit from the trees.

But then in chapter three Adam and Eve get into trouble. Because they eat of the tree of the knowledge of good and evil, God declares...

> Cursed is the ground because of you; through painful toil you will eat food from it all the days of your life. It will produce thorns and thistles for you, and you will eat the plants of the field. By the sweat of your brow you will eat your food until you return to the ground, since from it you were taken; for dust you are and to dust you will return. Genesis 3:17-19

What drama! In the first three chapters, God makes everything good and blessed, including us in His image. But then sin enters in. Adam and Eve break the one rule, and the ground gets cursed. Notice in the passage above, however, that the **ground is cursed, but the work is still blessed.**

Having talked to thousands of people for over 40 years about their work, I think most people believe that work is cursed. They even describe the beginning of the week as Monday Morning Blues and celebrate the end of the week with "Thank God It's Friday!"

WORK IS WORSHIP

The same word that is translated in the Old Testament as "work" can also be translated as "worship." In Genesis 2:15, when it says, "The Lord God took the man and put him in the garden of Eden to **work** it and take care of it," the word "work" is the Hebrew word transliterated as *abad*. In Psalms 102:22 the same word is used where it says, "... peoples gather together, and kingdoms, to **worship** the LORD." Work is worship.

From the very beginning, God made us to work as an act of worship. First and foremost, we are worshippers, not just workers. Do you think of your work as a call to worship?

I think most people think of work in one of three ways:

Job: work that a person does regularly in order to earn money; or a duty, task, or function.

Career: a series of jobs. According to *dictionary.com*, it means "an occupation or profession, especially one requiring special training followed as one's life work."

Calling: from the Greek word *kaleo*, which means "to call anyone, invite, summon." It refers primarily to a divine call as it relates to a vocation or redemption.

The truth is that work is not a job, career, or calling. It is all three together. If you start with thinking of work as a job, independent of being a calling, then work becomes drudgery—no purpose, no sense of fulfillment, no meaning, no mission.

But we were created in God's image from the beginning with the assignment of ruling over the world through the work of multiplying, filling, and subduing. Through the finished work of Jesus, we are still called to overcome in our work:

> I have told you these things, so that in me you may have peace. In this world you will have trouble. But take heart! I have overcome the world.
> John 16:33

GOOD WORKS DONE WELL

Good works are defined in two ways. First, good works are prepared by God for you to walk in. Secondly, you do a good job of whatever assignment He gives.

Now, consider what the Bible says about our attitude toward work:

> Obey those who are your masters on earth, not with external service, as those who merely please men, but with sincerity of heart, fearing the Lord. Whatever you do, do your work heartily, as for the Lord rather than for men, knowing that from the Lord you will receive the reward of the inheritance. It is the Lord Christ whom you serve. Colossians 3:22-24, NASB

Good works are not determined by merely external factors. Works are also made good when we work wholeheartedly for the Lord. The issue is not only what work you are doing, but how you are doing it.

A friend once came to me with his struggles at work. He felt that his boss was unreasonable and overly demanding. He proceeded to tell me this story:

> My boss is constantly on my case. He thinks my office is a mess, that I make personal calls on company time, and that I am always late. What he doesn't understand is that to the untrained eye my desk might look like a mess, but I know exactly where everything is. I might make a personal call here and there during the work day and occasionally I have been known to slide in a little late, but I stay late every day to make up for it, so it shouldn't matter to him as long as I am getting the work done, right?

I understood his plight. It was not the first time I had heard this similar story. Can you guess what advice I gave him? It was simple: clean up your office, quit making personal calls during the day, and arrive on time—or better yet—early. I asked him to implement these changes over the next 30 days, and then we would revisit the issue of his unreasonable boss.

Can you imagine what happened 30 days later? He and his boss were changed men. My friend honored his boss and the boss was pleased! The issue wasn't the boss or even the work. The issue was how my friend did the work.

WE ALL NEED HELP

Imagine an interview that lasts three hours and begins with this question?

"Would you tell me about yourself from the day after birth until this morning?"

I started asking that question when interviewing final candidates who had applied to be an independent operator of a Chick-fil-A restaurant. Each store was a huge investment of time, money, and effort. We believed that there was no more critical decision than selecting the right person. As we considered the experience and abilities of each candidate, we would also be thinking, "Would I want one of my children working for this person?"

Each candidate received the same parameters for answering.

"I am looking for the important things in your life. They are things you did and things that happened to you. They are usually the highest of highs and the lowest of lows in your life. Let's start with the day after your birth, you were... "

This one question became a conversation that took about an hour. As I guided candidates through their history, we explored events, relationships, accomplishments, and disappointments that they had perhaps not thought about in years. Often laughter and sometimes tears punctuated our dialogue. I prayed in my mind for enlightenment as theme lines and gut tugs came and went.

Other important questions included...

"As you look forward, what are your goals?" which I usually asked in the second hour. Each objective was explored for purpose and meaning.

In the third hour I asked, "Let's pretend! We are both 84 years old. We both know you will die in a few moments, and so I ask, '**As you look back over all of your life, what was really important?**'" Most candidates paused and reflected as they imagined and evaluated their lives running to the end.

The details of interviews were not only confidential, but they were treasured. The privilege of peeking into someone's life was an honor to be guarded and cherished.

Most precious of all was to see how God was working in and through each life, whether the candidate actually believed in Him or not. I could see that each and everyone one of us is "fearfully and wonderfully made."

I also discovered that God cares about every minute of everyone's whole life from beginning to end, including the work with which He occupies them from birth through death.

CAREER PLANNING GOD'S WAY

Joseph is an incredible example of career planning God's way. You can see how much God is involved from start to finish no matter how wild and wooly his life and career turned out to be. It is a great read starting in Genesis 37.

Here's a brief synopsis:

- *Born the favored son of rich farmer*
- *From shepherd to slave*
- *From slave to overseer of captain's household*
- *From overseer to falsely accused prisoner*
- *From prisoner to deputy warden and dream interpreter*
- *From prison to prime minister of the most powerful country in the world.*

Each step of the way God's sovereign plan was being fulfilled. Time and again, all seemed lost. From the pit to the prison, Joseph's career trajectory was not always straight up. Ultimately Joseph was in the right place – Pharoah's prison – at the right time – before a famine. God used Joseph's natural gifts and passions to do something truly monumental.

As a result of Joseph's careful planning and rise to power, he was able to bring his father and his reconciled family to Egypt to live under his care and protection, preserving the Israelites and ultimately preparing the way for Christ.

So many lessons from God showing up to Joseph responding, but the main point I want to make is that it was God at work throughout Joseph's life—regardless of circumstances or jobs assigned.

Walking in good works doesn't always feel like destiny. **Dreams coming true don't always feel like a dream-come-true.** As a young man Joseph dreamed about the sun, moon, and stars bowing down to him, ultimately angering his jealous brothers and leading to his enslavement. I doubt he imagined this dream's fulfillment would come about through a pit and a prison. But God had good works prepared for him, and he was faithful to walk in them no matter what it looked like.

REFLECTION QUESTIONS

1. How can I raise awareness of the value that God places on work with my church, organization, or ministry?

2. In what ways can I connect the dots between God's view of work and the daily work experiences and scenarios of people I know in the church or wider community?

3. What is one spiritual next step from this chapter that I can share with others? What is one practical next step?

PART 2

Get Set

SEVEN STEPS UPWARD
INWARD AND OUTWARD

TO FIND JOBS, CAREERS,
AND GOD'S CALLING

CHAPTER 4

Upward
LOVE GOD COMPLETELY

In Part 1, we talked about why the Church should help people find jobs, careers, and God's calling. The next three chapters outline "the what" of Christ-centered career ministry, which is the 7-step process we use in ministering to people through the Crossroads Career Network.

It will help you to consider what these seven steps may mean personally.

- *Are you clear about God's calling in your life?*
- *How are you developing your career?*
- *Are you prepared if you have to search for a new job?*

SEVEN STEPS TO NEXT

Whether people are unemployed or underemployed, misemployed, miserably employed, happily employed, or wondering about God's calling, everyone can walk seven steps successfully through crossroads in their careers:

1. Upward	God's calling
2. Attitude	Reach forward
3. Aptitude	Discover your best
4. Altitude	Target opportunities
5. Searching	Seek to serve
6. Sorting	Wow interviewers
7. Selecting	Walk in good works

These seven steps are the building blocks of a career ministry. Individuals who lose their jobs, hate their jobs, or have lost a sense of significance in the midst of their jobs can use these steps to assess where they're at, where God's calling them, and what they need to do next.

Get your own copy of our Crossroads Career Work Book: 7 Steps to Jobs, Career, and God's Calling at www.CrossroadsCareer.org/Store.

The first step – Upward – is to **hear and follow the upward calling of God.** It is a continuing invitation to love the Lord completely as He loves you. You can learn to talk with Him and walk with Him all day, every day.

Steps two through four – Inward – are about **planning your work**. They cluster together to help you develop your career in the light of God's calling. Positive attitude generates movement. Clarity about your aptitude gives you direction. Attitude plus aptitude gives your career an upward altitude, helping you search for and see opportunities God has prepared for you.

Steps five through seven – Outward – are about **working your plan.** Whether you desire to do your job better, advance your career, or press further toward the prize of the upward call of God, seek to serve others. Wow them with the love of a hearing heart. Walk in the heavenly vision with wisdom, strength, and courage.

Step 1 - Upward

The primary goal of career ministry is to help individuals hear and follow God's calling. With all the demands of every day, it is easy to get distracted and start focusing on people, places, and things that present themselves as problems or opportunities. Instead, we must teach people to turn their eyes upon Jesus, who summed up all the Law and the Prophets in these two commandments...

> "Love the Lord your God with all your heart and with all your soul and with all your mind." This is the first and greatest commandment. And the second is like it: "Love your neighbor as yourself." Matthew 22:37-39

Oz Guinness in his book *The Call* describes it this way:

> "Calling is the truth that God calls us to Himself so decisively that everything we are, everything we do, and everything we have is invested with a special devotion, dynamism, and direction lived out as a response to His summons and service."[1]

All of a sudden you are not just seeking to enhance your career or get and do a better job. You are learning to hear and follow God's calling, which transforms you to see who you are and Whose you are. Then you become empowered to seek and serve others who need most what God has given you.

Imagine everyone in your church more fully realizing his or her gifts, passions, and calling. If you're the pastor, include yourself in "everyone." Think of yourself as an explorer—ready for adventure. You are not too young, not too old. It is never too late. You are not stuck in muck. Challenges and opportunities in your church and life can bring out the best in you, and the best for you.

The upward journey is an exciting one. When you're on an upward trajectory, you'll open yourself to discovering new gifts and passions rather than relying on the familiar and routine. You'll develop a willingness to find new and better ways to do your job, exploring how your strengths can bring greater value to others while also making room for their strengths and talents.

Moving upward, you'll meet new people and make new friends, finding help, hope, and fellowship. You'll learn to count your blessings, reprioritize what is important, and recommit yourself to drawing nearer to God and His plans for your life.

But be warned: the upward journey will change you. You will be transformed from the inside out. And just like Moses after his journey up the mountain, you will come back looking different, maybe even shining a little bit.

Over the years of ministering to thousands of people, I keep hearing about 11 things that help them hear and follow God's calling. It is not an exhaustive list, it's not the only list, nor is it a formula for fellowship with God—it's just 11 things I have observed helping people to stay engaged with their calling. Just for fun, read each one and check those that you do at least once a week. Whatever you are not doing, you might try them out weekly for a month. See what happens.

1. Worship God

There is no calling without a Caller, so take dedicated time to worship, glorify, praise, and thank Him. As you live and work every day from waking until sleeping, do everything to honor Him.

> Ascribe to the LORD the glory due his name; worship... in the splendor of his holiness. Psalm 29:2

2. Read and Study the Bible

It's essential for you to know that the Bible is God's authority and our manual for living, so stop seeing it as a dusty old document and consider it as bread, and feed from it every day. If you have never read the Bible, consider starting with the book of John, Ephesians, or Psalms.

> Your word is a lamp for my feet, a light on my path. Psalm 119:105

3. Pray

Learn how essential it is to converse with God every day, perhaps multiple times during every day. This habit teaches two things: first, He is always available, and second, we need His constant guidance. You may be unfamiliar with prayer, so use a psalm as your own personal prayer.

> Show me the way I should go, for to you I entrust my life. Psalm 143:8

4. Listen to God

Prayer is two-way communication. Listen and write thoughts that come to mind in a journal or notebook for later reflection and Bible study.

> Be still, and know that I am God. Psalm 46:10

5. Be with Christians

This revelation can change someone's life: you need to spend time with Christians that you like and who like you. Study the Bible together. Pray together. Encourage one another. Follow the ABCs of Accountability, Belonging, and Care.

> Consider how we may spur one another on toward love and good deeds.
> Hebrews 10:24

6. Seek Wise Counsel

People often get in career ruts due to prideful independence. The practice of seeking wisdom first from above (James 3:17) and then from other people helps you make better decisions.

> Let the wise listen and add to their learning, and let the discerning get
> guidance. Proverbs 1:5

7. Consider Unfolding Circumstances

It is easy to miss what's right in front of you, so we teach the importance of being a good steward of the opportunities God gives you, considering each situation with God in prayer.

> Be very careful, then, how you live... making the most of every opportunity.
> Ephesians 5:15-16

8. Confess and Clear Your Head

A clear head is critical in thinking through options and seeking God's leading. It is easy to become confused, especially if sin is getting in the way. The solution is to confess it and clear it out every day.

> If we confess our sins, He is faithful and righteous to forgive us our sins and
> to cleanse us . . . . 1 John 1:9, NASB

9. Be Alert for God's Peace

For a follower of Christ, peace is like a compass, so be alert for the peace that transcends all understanding as you consider various options and paths. It helps forge the way even in the midst of the most chaotic of times.

> And the peace of God, which transcends all understanding, will guard your hearts and your minds in Christ Jesus. Philippians 4:7

10. Keep a Journal

Many have found it helpful to keep track of what they learn from their Bible reading, thoughts they have during prayer, advice they receive from their friends, unfolding circumstances, and things that bring God's peace.

> This is what the Lord says . . . "Write all the words which I have spoken to you in a book." Jeremiah 30:2, NASB

11. Trust and Obey

There is no other way! If you think the Lord wants you to do something, and it seems to be in alignment with everything we have been talking about, then do it! If you hear Him, follow Him.

> Whoever has my commands and keeps them is the one who loves me. The one who loves me will be loved by my Father, and I too will love them and show myself to them. John 14:21

IT PAINS ME TO WRITE THIS...

It pains me to write this, but I understand that there are ministry leaders—and even pastors—who do not really know Jesus. They know about Him, study Him, and read His words, but they don't know Him. Consider these verses ...

> Not everyone who says to Me, "Lord, Lord," will enter the kingdom of heaven, but he who does the will of My Father who is in heaven will enter. Many will say to Me on that day, "Lord, Lord, did we not prophesy in Your name, and in Your name cast out demons, and in Your name perform many miracles?" And then I will declare to them, "I never knew you; depart from Me, you who practice lawlessness. Matthew 7:21–23, NASB

If you think He might not know you, because you don't experientially know Him, I have very good news! God, who created the world and everything in it, wants to have a personal relationship with you. He made it possible by His Son paying the price for your sin—the only thing that separates you from Him. By accepting His Son as payment on your behalf, you can have a relationship with the Creator of the universe, starting now and for eternity.

> For God so loved the world that he gave his one and only Son, that
> whoever believes in him shall not perish but have eternal life.
> John 3:16

Even in the midst of the agony of defeat, it is possible to experience victory.
You can discover that God is good. God is great. Seek Him and His righteousness, and all the other things He has prepared will be added to you.

God is not only calling you to salvation, but also to sanctification and service—
in that order all the time. Work out your faith in Him upward, inward, and
outward. He made you for good works.

Upward	**Salvation**
Inward	**Sanctification**
Outward	**Service**

CAREER VS. CALLING?

Career, according to *dictionary.com*, means "an occupation or profession, especially one requiring special training, followed as one's lifework."

Calling comes from the Greek *kaleo*, which means "to call anyone, invite, summon." It refers primarily to a divine call as it relates to a vocation or redemption.

How do these concepts fit together? For some people, it's one or the other. A
pastor would probably say my work is a calling, not a career. Someone in the
congregation might tell you he has a career but is not sure about a calling.

Let me propose that **everyone should have both a career and a calling.** They
are not mutually exclusive terms. One, however, should be first. As you might
guess, I vote for calling, then career flows out of your following Him.

But I also hasten to add there is a subtle, but critical, difference between God's
calling and your calling. When you think the words "my calling," odds are you
are talking about your thoughts based on your passions and gifts. Terrible mistake! You are likely focused inward with little love upward.

Refocus upward and ask "What is Your calling for me today, Lord?" God is not
only calling you to a manifest destiny, but also to many individual steps along
the way. Consider how God called Abraham...

By faith Abraham, when he was called, obeyed by going out to a place which he was to receive for an inheritance; and he went out, not knowing where he was going. By faith he lived as an alien in the land of promise, as in a foreign land, dwelling in tents with Isaac and Jacob, fellow heirs of the same promise; for he was looking for the city which has foundations, whose architect and builder is God. Hebrews 11:8-10, NASB

So, do not be upset that you are going out not knowing where you are going. By faith, know Who you are following! Maybe that is why God had the Holy Spirit stimulate Paul to write these verses...

Rejoice always, pray continually, give thanks in all circumstances.
1 Thessalonians 5:16-18

Wow! Now that is a challenge. Pray, rejoice and give thanks all the time in everything? That is just not possible. Why would I even try?

... for this is God's will for you in Christ Jesus. 1 Thessalonians 5:18

REFLECTION QUESTIONS

1. On a scale of one to ten, how well do you think the average person in your church or organization understands their calling? Also on a scale of one to ten, how intently are they pursuing their calling?

2. How can you help them move up one number on that scale?

3. What is one spiritual next step from this chapter that I can share with others in my church or on my team? What is one practical next step?

CHAPTER 5

Inward
LOVE YOURSELF CORRECTLY

As you walk through the next three steps – Attitude, Aptitude and Altitude – you begin to be transformed. As you take an inward journey, the truth of how you are God's masterpiece created in Christ Jesus for good works changes your inner attitudes and outward actions. For many people it is the first time they begin to love themselves correctly, as God see them.

Attitude is about building a positive, Christ-centered perspective to overcome anger, fear, and depression. Aptitude is discovering your best - not only your gifts but also your passions and calling. Altitude is learning how to target opportunities by identifying who needs most what you do best.

Attitude plus Aptitude gives your job search and career development Altitude, all connected to Christ in the center. Can you imagine the transformation that begins to take place in you, your family, and in your church?

Step 2 - Attitude

Imagine a church full of people who consider it pure joy to get up and go to work every morning. That kind of attitude is noticed by bosses and colleagues alike, and it has a real impact on productivity and wellbeing for everyone. But few of us wake up with this outlook, and so we have the opportunity to improve our attitude to the positive.

> "Most folks are about as happy as they make up their minds to be."
> Abraham Lincoln

Let's try a little exercise. Rate your attitude on a scale of one to ten—one being down in the dumps, ten being on top of the world. Got your number? Honest? If you need to think about it I can wait... Once you got your number, write it down, and ask yourself: "Why did I give myself that number? Why did I withhold points? Why did I give myself any points at all?"

Odds are that your attitude reflects your circumstances. If your situation is good, bad, or ugly, then it is likely that your attitude is correspondingly good, bad, or ugly. Bad situations breed bad feelings. **A positive attitude turns stumbling blocks into building blocks.** You feel better. You think better. You even look better. Is it possible to be in The Pit circumstantially, yet live each day with joy?

Okay, now I want you to do something. Take the number you gave yourself, and add one to it. Go ahead... cross out the number you wrote and add one to it. There, you've just improved your attitude!

> Forgetting what lies behind and reaching forward to what lies ahead, I press on toward the goal for the prize of the upward call of God in Christ Jesus. Philippians 3:13-14, NASB

Look at each word carefully. You will discover three Biblical principles for building a positive attitude.

- *"Forgetting what lies behind"* is about accepting loss and overcoming anger.
- *"Reaching forward to what lies ahead"* is about accepting opportunity and vaporizing fear.
- *"Pressing toward the goal of the prize of the upward call of God"* requires strength training, which will help you defeat depression.

Imagine the impact this kind of teaching and equipping has on members of your congregation and in outreach to your community. Every step of the way is Scripture, truth, and application. Such information and inspiration with application brings transformation.

Let's look more deeply at these three Biblical principles.

FORGET WHAT LIES BEHIND

Ever lose something very important? You will find freedom to move to the future if you admit, understand, and grieve the loss, no matter how minor or major it may be. Loss, hurt, disappointment, and injustice are all roads that lead to the same destination: anger.

If you haven't experienced job loss lately, it may be hard to relate, but it's a very frustrating experience. The emotional toll can be staggering, sometimes to the point that the person can't see beyond his or her own anger. **Anger is just one**

letter short of danger. That's why it is important to "not let the sun go down on your anger" (Ephesians 4:26).

Here are some common symptoms associated with the emotional setbacks of joblessness:

- *Denial: This can't be. I don't believe it!*
- *Panic: What do I do? How do I handle this?*
- *Anger: They can't do that to me! I will get them!*
- *Depression: I'm tired and don't feel like doing anything.*
- *Stress: I don't feel well/headache/stomachache.*

As you admit your feelings about your situation, you may feel that you have been used, abused, and refused. Maybe you are blaming others or maybe even yourself.

Everyone feels anger sometimes. It's what you do next that counts. These steps can be useful in extinguishing the flames.

1. *Describe the offense and how you feel about it.*

2. *List everyone you blame. The list may include yourself or even God.*

3. *Exercise forgiveness, because God forgives you.*

I use the word exercise, because forgiveness is not an event. It is a process that might take years to dissolve the hurt, pain, and grip of anger. Just let go of your anger, and anger will let go of you. You *can* put the past behind you.

REACH FORWARD TO WHAT LIES AHEAD

This is the first day of the rest of your life. Make decisions now for the better that will last forever. Start by asking yourself:

- *When I look back at the end of my life, what will be important?*
- *Am I on the planet for a purpose? What is it?*
- *How does God see my life?*

See a future for yourself in which you are not only maximizing your career, but you are experiencing an overall sense of wellbeing. Consider goals that begin with Christ in the center of your soul for your whole life. Imagine your highest felt needs for family, friends, health, wealth, and work.

Begin to picture your work and calling in ways in which you are content, fulfilled, and in alignment with God's will. Make plans and think about what it will take to accomplish them one step at a time.

"For I know the plans I have for you," declares the Lord, "plans to prosper
you and not to harm you, plans to give you hope and a future."
Jeremiah 29:11, NASB

I am all about the hope, but I get nervous about the future both near and far
away.

I remember being in the headquarters parking lot of a prospective client. With
ten minutes to go before the meeting, anxiety teased me. I reached for my Bible
on the front seat. As a new Christian only a few months old, I did not know
where to turn, so I just prayed and then blindly opened to the page with these
verses...

Be anxious for nothing, but in everything by prayer and supplication with
thanksgiving, let your requests be made known to God. And the peace of
God, which surpasses all comprehension, will guard your hearts and your
minds in Christ Jesus. Philippians 4:6-7, NASB

Prayer answered immediately. God gave me peace that surpassed my understanding. Even though I did not get the business, it was a great meeting, because I experienced God getting me.

When King Solomon interviewed David for the Goliath fight, David looked into
the past to recount stories of God's protection and provision, describing his experiences of fighting off bears and lions. Then he predicted that the God who
rescued him from bear and the lion would also help him defeat this Philistine.

David got the job and a new career. He saw God in his life—past, present, and
future. He looked fearlessly at Goliath in the light of God's size and strength.
Nothing is too great for you and God.

For God hath not given us the spirit of fear; but of power, and of love, and
of a sound mind. 2 Timothy 1:7, KJV

PRESS ON TOWARD THE UPWARD CALL

"Pressing on" requires personal strength training, which creates much needed
energy and endurance. You will need to build yourself up for the journey ahead.
With strength comes courage. Consider a personal strength-training program.
Eat right, exercise, and get plenty of rest, not only physically, but also mentally and spiritually.

Physically: Pay attention to nutrition; cut calories and fat; reduce caffeine and
alcohol. Exercise three to five times a week, if a doctor approves. Get at least
seven hours of sleep a night.

CREATED FOR GOOD WORKS | 61

> But I discipline my body and make it my slave, so that, after I have
> preached to others, I myself will not be disqualified.
> 1 Corinthians 9:27, NASB

Mentally: Renew your mind, will, and emotions in Jesus with open hands, gentle touch, and a hearing heart. Feed your mind good words, sounds, and pictures. Spend time with good friends. Do things you enjoy. Also take time to do nothing, and give your brain a break.

> And do not be conformed to this world, but be transformed by the
> renewing of your mind, so that you may prove what the will of God is, that
> which is good and acceptable and perfect. Romans 12:2, NASB

Spiritually: Be intimate with God an hour a day, one day every week, and one week per quarter. Memorize, meditate, and master Ephesians or some other great book. Get together with others for mutual Bible study and prayer. And when God calls you to stop, then stop ...

> But those who hope in the Lord will renew their strength. They will soar on
> wings like eagles; they will run and not grow weary; they will walk and not
> be faint. Isaiah 40:31

Can you see how attitudes in your church – not just at work, but also in life – will change to be more positive? Could it be because the people your church is ministering to are seeing more of Jesus, and not just jobs?

HELP FOR OTHER PRESSURE POINTS

The reason I am so excited when a local church starts helping people find jobs, careers, and God's calling is that most churches have all the other helping ministries.

People often experience money problems along with work issues. Benevolence and financial ministries can help bring balance and relieve stress. If people don't have a budget, then they can make one. If they have debt, they can add it up and pay it down. The less income they need, the more freedom they have to accept the job God has reserved for them. A good job with good income is a good platform for giving to the church.

Work and money problems can wreck a good marriage and family. Husbands and wives can wind up at odds with each other, instead of loving, respecting, and supporting one another. Communication, collaboration, and commitment are critical components to working together. Churches usually have internal or external resources and counsel for families in crisis. Marriage ministries can help spouses to not withdraw, but rather stay connected not only to each other, but also to family, friends, and church.

Pastors and church leaders are usually equipped to support people with their personal issues. Job loss and career dissatisfaction often erode personal confidence. Church small groups as well as pastoral counseling can provide much needed encouragement and positive stimulation. With the help of the church, members can reset their attitudes to the next highest levels.

In our church, we focus on five discipleship functions: worship, connect, serve, give, and invite. With everyone connected to someone, the church can exhibit the love of God upward, inward, and outward. We are all better together – rejoicing, praying, and giving thanks.

Step 3 - Aptitude

There is no one like you anywhere. Never has been. Never will be. You are uniquely designed by God. No other person on the planet has your DNA and personal history. No doubt you know this verse...

> For You created my inmost being; you knit me together in my mother's womb. I praise you because I am fearfully and wonderfully made.
> Psalm 139:13-14, NASB

YOUR UNIQUE DESIGN

Let's continue to think about you as God's workmanship. You were designed for a specific purpose that only you can fulfill. This distinctive role causes you to reflect a unique aspect of God's glory. The better you understand you, the better you can see how to maximize your career. Consider these six factors of your unique design:

1. **Experiences:** *Your background - personal, educational, vocational*

2. **Abilities:** *What you do best - talents, knowledge, skills*

3. **Personality:** *How you do best what you do best - natural behaviors*

4. **Interests:** *What you like best - people, places, things, activities you enjoy*

5. **Values:** *What is important—your work and life purpose and principles*

6. **Factor X:** *The presence and power of the Holy Spirit, who manifests spiritual gifts and calling.*

As a follower of Christ, you get one extra factor: The X-factor. It's the active presence of Jesus Christ in your life. It begins the moment you are created anew in Christ Jesus by accepting Him as your Savior and Lord.

Therefore if anyone is in Christ, he is a new creature; the old things passed away; behold, new things have come. 2 Corinthians 5:17, NASB

Your experiences, abilities, and personality are your gifts. Interests and values together become your passions. Your gifts and passions, ignited by the Holy Spirit, are transformed into spiritual gifts and calling, not only in church and ministry, but also in your every day life at home and work.

Even as a talking, walking Christian, I went a lot of years trying to do things for God on my own, without being aware of the Holy Spirit and the important role He could play in my life. I was aware of my gifts and passions, but it never occurred to me that they might become supernatural!

You are made on purpose for a purpose to do good works. Your experiences, abilities, and personality combine with your interests and values and are then multiplied by the Holy Spirit for work God has prepared.

As each one has received a special gift, employ it in serving one another as good stewards of the manifold grace of God. 1 Peter 4:10, NASB

What does it mean "special gift"? According to *Strong's Exhaustive Concordance and Dictionary*, the definition includes... "Grace or gifts denoting extraordinary powers, distinguishing certain Christians and enabling them to serve the church of Christ, the reception of which is due to the power of divine grace operating on their souls by the Holy Spirit."

What does it mean to you to employ your gifts in service to others as a good steward of the manifold grace of God? Your work has a two-fold effect. Horizontally, you serve others on earth. Vertically, you glorify your Father in heaven.

EMPLOY PASSIONS, AS WELL AS GIFTS

As you think about yourself uniquely designed by God for His glory, also consider how you can encourage your church staff and congregation to think about their gifts and passions.

Researchers followed a group of people over a period of twenty years. Most of the people started off their career path by choosing to do whatever made them the most money now so that they would be free to do what they wanted later in life. But a much smaller group was full of individuals who decided to do what they love now and to figure out the money later.

At the end of the 20-year period, 101 of the 1,500 subjects had become millionaires. You'll never guess which group produced the most millionaires. All but one of them came from the group who chose a career path doing what they loved rather than what paid the most.[1]

Education, goals, plans ... those are all well and good. But your passions are uniquely you, and they'll drive you to work harder than external reward.

DISCOVER AND DEVELOP YOUR BEST

It's a good idea to be intentional in uncovering the six factors of your unique design, and to do so we have found three approaches to be very fruitful.

First, do self-assessment. Inventory your job and employer experiences, your accomplishments, and keywords that you think describe you.

Second, ask others to give you feedback. Ask people from work, school, family, and friends about your experiences, accomplishments, abilities, values, interests, and personality.

Third, take advantage of a variety of professional assessments that will identify or describe your abilities, personality, interests, values, and spiritual gifts.

Doing these assessments and then summarizing what you learned in terms of your gifts, passions, and calling can help you to develop and discover your best.

You have natural strengths and weaknesses. Once upon a time, training focused on everyone being good at everything, which meant that you worked extra hard trying to make your natural weaknesses stronger. The problem was no matter how much training you got, if you were not talented in a particular area, you would never be great!

Today, more attention is being paid to identifying your talents—your most natural thoughts, feelings, and behaviors. Your talents are foundational and reflected in your personality, interests, values, spiritual gifts, and calling. Add knowledge and skills to your talents to build and become your personal best.

Do you think of yourself as God's masterpiece? Consider again these two commandments...

> You shall love the Lord your God with all your heart and with all your soul and with all your mind. This is the great and first commandment. And a second is like it: You shall love your neighbor as yourself. On these two commandments depend all the Law and the Prophets.
> Matthew 22:37-40, NASB

Did you skip over the part where it reads that you are supposed to love yourself? Here is what author Ken Boa in his book *Face to Face* writes about how you can love yourself...

"To love ourselves correctly is to see ourselves as God sees us and to allow the Word, not the world, to define who and whose we really are. The clearer we capture the vision of our new identity in Jesus Christ, the more we will realize that our deepest needs for security, significance, and satisfaction are met in Him and not in people, possessions, or positions."[2]

Prayerfully discovering your six factors can help you change the way you see yourself to be more in alignment with how God sees you. **When you see a better picture of how you're made, you have a better understanding of what you're made for.**

As you explore how you are made in God's image, imagine members of your congregation and community discovering the marks of being made master-pieces. Most people do not fully appreciate whose they are, what they can do, and the purpose for doing good works. Just this past Saturday I watched to an unemployed woman speak with clarity and confidence about how she realized her value. The prior week she enjoyed two promising interviews because she was receiving what God was doing in her and was able to reflect that in other areas of her life.

Step 4 - Altitude

A positive Attitude, plus clarity about your Aptitude, will lift your Altitude.

When you recognize that you are God's masterpiece and that the characteristics He has given you have purpose and that you can know what that is, you can begin to look for ways to find those who need most what you do best.

Meditate on this:

> As each one has received a special gift, employ it in serving one another as good stewards of the manifold grace of God. 1 Peter 4:10, NASB

Just as there are six factors to Aptitude, there are also six factors to think, pray, and explore in targeting opportunities for serving others. The good news is that there is a wealth of resources available to help sort through occupations, employers, locations, income, platforms, and culture.

Occupations

This is the work you do that occupies your time and hopefully your talent. In job descriptions, occupations are described as responsibilities, duties, tasks, and activities.

For much more information, you can explore O*Net *(www.onetonline.org)*, my favorite source of occupational information with more than 1,000 listings.

For members of your congregation seeking new or different careers, they can identify possibilities with keyword searches on O*Net. It's a little bit like searching for gold, shoveling lots of dirt before finding potential veins of value, but made easier with the click of a mouse. For every occupation found, there are descriptions of work activities, abilities, interests, education needed, wages, and employment, with additional links.

Employers

These are the people and organizations for which you do the work. Employers are organized in groups called industries. If you are a pastor, more than likely you work for a church, although there are other Christian and ministry organizations that might employ you, including businesses that hire corporate chaplains.

There are literally millions of employers looking to hire from employees to executives. To make things more manageable, you and members of your church can research more than 100 major industry groups for occupations, wages, and trends. Visit the Bureau of Labor Statistics website for "Industries at a Glance."

Don't forget employers in your congregation and community who are seeking candidates for jobs. Many churches receive job postings from local employers big and small. As they are reaching into your congregation to fill jobs, you can connect with them with the good news of Jesus. Becoming members of chambers of commerce and other community organizations can be an effective and practical outreach for evangelism of the community and care for your congregation.

Locations

Where you work matters.

Pastors and ministry leaders are just as susceptible to the possibilities of moving as their congregational members. It might be relocation for a new job, to take care of family, or to fulfill personal preferences of a better lifestyle or economic climate.

Maybe relocation is not necessary, but constant travel is required. Some of my friends in sales hop a plane on Monday morning and hope to be home for dinner on Friday.

Commuting is more common then you think. The wife of one of my ministry partners happily lives at home in Georgia, but works in California – glamorously called bicoastal.

Another buddy shared with me this conversation with his wife: "Honey, I got an offer to be director of marketing for ABC company in New Jersey." She replied, "Sweetheart, I married you for better or for worse, but not for New Jersey."

My marketing friend took a job in New York City and bought a home on the Georgia coast. Friday to Monday he is in sandals on the sand. Monday through Thursday he's walking in wingtips on the pavement.

Making work location decisions can be complicated. To make things simpler and safer before you relocate or start commuting to other locations in the United States, go to *www.bestplaces.net*. For exploring other countries, explore world missions or relief organizations. Believe it or not, another great resource about other countries is the CIA's World Fact Book website.

Income

Decisions about work are always about money, and always about more than money.

Income may consist of wages, salary, commissions, bonuses, and/or tips. Also take into consideration benefits such as medical, life, and disability insurance, as well retirement plans. It is best to be as flexible as possible by reducing your cost of living as much as you can, especially if you are changing careers during which time you may earn less as you learn a new occupation or industry. To find out how much jobs pay, go to *www.salary.com*.

For yourself as pastor or advising others, always take and give this advice. Lower your cost of living, and set right priorities in your financial life. First, give generously to the Lord. Next, meet your obligations for paying taxes and eliminating debt. Next is to build your savings. Finally, spend as little as possible on day-to-day living. Your living expenses should meet your need, not your greed.

Platforms

You may not know that there are actually four basic platforms upon which most people work:

- *Employee*
- *Independent contractor*
- *Business owner*
- *Volunteer*

You are an employee if the employer can control what will be done and how it will be done. You are a contractor if your employer has the right to control or direct the result of the work done, but not the means and methods of accomplishing the result. Maybe you're an owner with your own business, or maybe you want to be an owner. Or perhaps you're a volunteer who believes in what the organization is doing or really like the work you are doing.

As you know, most of the work in many churches is done by volunteers. If you are starting or changing careers and need experience, volunteering or doing free internships are great ways to learn skills and build contacts. In the new world of work, it is wise to be flexible and open to all four different working platforms.

Culture

Organizational culture reflects the operating values of employers, including churches. Research shows that matching your personal values to the organization and individual for whom you work is the number one issue in job satisfaction and work engagement. Or said another way, most people quit a job because of the boss.

A pastor who struggles in a church is probably not synced up with the hierarchy of the denomination or the church board of elders, deacons, or trustees. Members of your congregation can have the same culture-values problems whether they are working for an employer or are serving customers.

Whether you are a pastor in the wrong church culture or you are counseling a member of your congregation, be sensitive to the individual values and organizational culture fit.

Target Opportunities

Whether you are a pastor or member of a church, work has been prepared for you, and you can find it.

Seek to serve others with your gifts, passions, and calling. Explore all six factors to help target right opportunities.

Not all targeting factors have the same importance. For example, location might be most important because your family has a critical need. Or occupation and income may be more important than location or industry. Prioritize what factors you believe to be most essential.

Throughout this process, "be anxious for nothing, but in everything by prayer and petition with thanksgiving, let your requests be made known to God." You will know you are on the right path as you experience peace that surpasses all understanding in Christ Jesus.

Your message

Everyone must somehow, someway effectively communicate what they do best for people who need it most. To make it super simple, write a message plan with three parts...

- *Who needs most what you do best*
- *What you do best – gifts, passion, calling*
- *What are the results and benefits of your work*

Your message is how God is working in you and through you to others. It consists of a headline and a statement of value you deliver. The headline should be two to ten words designed to get someone's attention. For example, my personal headline is:

**Connect people to Christ
at decisive moments in their careers**

When I say those words to pastors and ministry leaders, they usually want to know more. I follow up with...

**Equip and support the Church
By providing Christ-centered resources
To help people find jobs, careers, and God's calling**

Once defined and refined, your message can and should be used everywhere: networking, resumes and bios, interviews, presentations, social media, blogs, business cards, and more. Start developing your message and practicing it with others. Pay attention to how they respond. If they respond with a "Wow," then start delivering the message using every available means.

DO WHAT YOU DO BEST

Do you have the opportunity at work to do what you do best every day? For most of us, the unfortunate answer is "No!"

In the United States, "the majority of American adults say they are not able to use their strengths to do what they do best throughout the day," according to 2012 Gallup research.[3]

You are God's unique masterpiece created for good works. How different would your work life be if you could do what you do and like best every day? You would be happier and more productive. Don't wait. Discover your best, and seek opportunities to serve where you work now.

MAKE BAD WORK BETTER

If you are anything less than fulfilled and fruitful as a ministry leader, you might be contributing to the problem.

If you are doing anything less than your very best, you are shortchanging yourself, the church, and God. If you have a bad attitude about your role, board, staff, ministry leaders, or any other aspect of your work, that attitude will affect your performance and relationships.

To maximize your calling, consider this:

> Whatever you do, work at it with all your heart, as working for the Lord, not for human masters, since you know that you will receive an inheritance from the Lord as a reward. It is the Lord Christ you are serving.
> Colossians 3:23-24

Does this describe you and how you work? Are you working heartily and with sincerity of heart? Are you serving God in your job? Maybe you are thinking, "Yeah, but you don't know about this church and its board." You're right, but consider this:

> Submit yourselves to your masters, not only to those who are good and considerate, but also to those who are harsh. 1 Peter 2:18

If "harsh" describes your boss or board, it is especially important to take your attitude and performance to their highest. You may discover your situation changes for the better when you modify how you are working.

STAY OR LEAVE?

Whether you decide to stay in or leave your current job, continue to love God completely upward, love yourself correctly inward, and love others compassionately outward.

If you stay in your current role, search for more people whom you can serve better. Sort through what they need and what you have to offer. Select carefully what you do for whom.

If you decide to leave, then search for people outside your current employment. Seek to serve those who need most what you do best. Let God work in and through you to transform your life, as you sort through new opportunities and select the one prepared for you.

Whether you decide to stay or leave, you can apply the three outward steps in the next chapter.

REFLECTION QUESTIONS

1. How would the career ministry building block of Attitude influence and potentially help the entire culture of my church?

2. How would the career ministry building block of Aptitude help me identify and apply the unique strengths and gifts of church members? How would it create some Altitude to affect our entire community?

3. What is one spiritual next step from this chapter that I can share with my church or team? What is one practical next step?

CHAPTER 6

Outward
LOVE OTHERS COMPASSIONATELY

As a pastor or ministry leader, you already know Jesus' command to love your neighbors with compassion.

As a shepherd in the Church, you are to care for and feed the sheep, just as Jesus instructed Peter.

If you've completed steps one through four, you've already positioned yourself to stop looking for a job or developing your career. Instead, you are following God's calling one step at a time.

Steps five through seven will help you take what you've learned so far and put it into action by searching for opportunities to serve, sorting through them, and selecting the ones God prepared for you, whether you stay in your current role or are led to search for something else.

Step 5 - Searching

You're searching for opportunities to serve others with your strengths, gifts, and passions. It's about giving, not getting. Whether you are looking to do better in the job you have, or you want a better job, listen to others with a hearing heart.

When you search, use both eyes. One eye is for looking according to your plan, and the other eye is for seeing as God directs. **Always be prayerful, intentional, and alert.**

> The mind of man plans his way, but the Lord directs his steps.
> Proverbs 16:9, NASB

Sometimes finding the right opportunity comes from seeing something you are not seeking. The best strategy combines three efforts:

> All-the-Time Praying
> +
> On-the-Ground Networking
> +
> Online Searching

ALL-THE-TIME PRAYING

It's a common mistake in the pursuit of our calling to start off by seeking God for vision and direction, and then turn to our own efforts to accomplish it. The One who began a good work is faithful to complete it. We can't do it without Him.

We encourage those in the searching process to imagine they are dialing 1-800-Dear-God, calling by prayer the one Person who knows everyone, everywhere, all the time. We can ask Him every day before every meeting, phone call, and email.

He knows the plans He has for you. He knows where all the opportunities are. He knows everyone who is looking for what you do. Consider this verse:

> Ask, and it will be given to you; seek, and you will find; knock, and the door will be opened to you. Matthew 7:7

It's amazing how just three minutes of putting this into practice can change everything. Just grab a journal, pray, listen for God's direction, and write down what you hear. You'll be surprised how often a simple idea will pop into your head—a person to call, an email to write, an opportunity to pursue—that can change the course of your day, or possibly even the course of your life.

ON-THE-GROUND NETWORKING

It's not just what you know, but also it's who you know. This is why personal referrals are the most effective way to find opportunities. Someone you know introduces you to someone they know. It could be in-person, by phone, via email and now through social media: Facebook, Twitter, LinkedIn. All of these media are extremely effective when you are seeking to serve.

If you are looking for a new job or a different career path, be aware that most employers first try to recruit people through their personal contacts before they advertise a position or post on the Internet. Most positions that get filled are never listed anywhere because of personal referrals. A startling statistic came from a private corporate study that demonstrated that applicants who had been personally referred were 42 times more likely to be selected than those without personal referrals. That's a 4,200% better chance!

Why is this true? First, the employer knows someone who knows you. Second, you are more likely to be favorably received because of the positive reputation of the referral. Third, the likelihood of a match between personal values and corporate culture is higher.

Amazing, isn't it? Most of the available opportunities are not listed anywhere. It is even truer for contract work and finding customers for your business. You can only find them through personal referrals. That is why we recommend that those looking for work spend 50% to 85% of their search time networking to make personal contacts, serve others, build relationships, and receive personal referrals.

Effective networking starts with helping other people first. **Seek to serve and add value to others.** It is more blessed to give than receive. If you help enough people get what they want, you will eventually get what you want. Combine a positive attitude, courtesy, and flexibility. Say what you will do and do what you say. Be creative, yet thoughtful of each person.

Imagine that you are on an elevator. Someone that you know gets on and asks about how you are doing. You say that you are doing great and you are looking for more opportunities to serve people with what you do. They reply with some version of "What do you do or what kind of opportunities do you seek?" You have less than thirty seconds to respond before the elevator doors open and your friend walks off.

Share your three-part strengths and value statement you developed for your, bio, CV or resume back in Step 4:

- **Part 1:** *Who needs most what you do best.*
- **Part 2:** *What you do best such as experiences, abilities, personality, interests, values, and spiritual gifts.*
- **Part 3:** *The value others receive from your work.*

Sharing the value you offer can take as little as ten seconds. You have time to answer questions and ask for referrals or a follow-up. Offer your personal card, and ask for theirs. You can use networking scripts whether you seek traditional employment, work as a contractor, or to start a business.

Once you start getting positive feedback, put keywords with your name and contact information on a personal business-size card.

ONLINE SEARCHING

Social networks can be a great way to make online connection and bridge to on-the-ground meetings.

Warning! Personal pages on social networking sites will likely be found by re-cruiters and employers who are considering you for a position. Be careful about the type of information and photos they might find. Good news! Networking sites can be a great place to plant good information about yourself. Create or modify your member profile that includes what you do best, your value, strengths, and accomplishments.

Search for key contacts who are currently or formerly with target employers us-ing social media sites, such as LinkedIn, Facebook, Twitter, or Instagram.

Searching isn't easy, but when you are working from the revelation that God made you for a purpose, and you seek to use that purpose to serve others, you'll find you're not alone in the hunt. By your side will be the One who prom-ised that you'll receive what you ask for, you'll find what you seek, and doors will open if you just keep knocking.

Step 6 - Sorting

Interviews consist of three underlying questions: "Who are you?" "What do you want?" "What can you do for me?"

Your goal is to "wow" the interviewer by seeking to serve whether you are a fit for the job or not.[1]

Contrary to conventional wisdom, most interviewing is actually two-way. In the world of sales calls, it's called qualifying a prospect and pitching a product or service. Again, it is asking questions and sharing information. Even dating is the same process of sifting and sorting whether there is potential mutual benefit to meeting up again.

Are you confident that your next interview will result in some sort of relation-ship? For most of us, the answer is probably no. In the process of job interview-ing, the success rates average about 10%. If you are hoping every conversation leads to a relationship of some kind, this could be really disappointing.

I think that is why Jesus uses agricultural illustrations to give you a feel for the odds.

> Behold, the sower went out to sow; and as he sowed, some seeds fell
> beside the road, and the birds came and ate them up. Others fell on the
> rocky places, where they did not have much soil; and immediately they
> sprang up, because they had no depth of soil. But when the sun had
> risen, they were scorched; and because they had no root, they withered

away. Others fell among the thorns, and the thorns came up and choked them out. And others fell on the good soil and yielded a crop, some a hundredfold, some sixty, and some thirty. He who has ears, let him hear.
Matthew 13:3-9, NASB

How great would it be if your interviewer concluded the meeting with "Wow! That was impressive!" Let's start with three basic principles of sorting through opportunities by interviewing and evaluating:

- *Help them connect what they need most with what you do best.*
- *People prefer people they like, so keep generating a positive attitude.*
- *Interviewing is a two-way street.*

ENGAGING INTERVIEWS

Consider four steps to increase interviewing success: Pray, Prepare, Perform, Praise.

PRAY: Start with your heart. Fill it with positive thoughts about how to serve the interests of the employer or customer with what you do and like best.

Dress for success spiritually. Prayerfully put on the full armor of God as described in Ephesians 6:10-17.

- *Belt girded with truth*
- *Breastplate of righteousness*
- *Shoes of gospel of peace*
- *Shield of faith*
- *Helmet of salvation*
- *Sword as the Word of God*

Spiritual "underwear" is more important than physical outerwear. Post this list where you will see it when you dress. Remember to put on the full armor of God. Don't leave home without it!

Remember, whatever put in your heart will show up on your lips.

PREPARE: When you go to an interview, you want to demonstrate that you are prepared, passionate, and also qualified.[2]

Demonstrate how you are qualified by sharing relevant STAR stories about what God has accomplished in and through you in your life and work so far.

- *What was the Situation you faced?*
- *What was the Task to be accomplished?*
- *What were the Actions you took?*
- *What were the Results you got?*

Research the employer or customer by visiting their website to read and print information about who they are, what they do, recent news, careers, and their jobs. Search the Internet for more information. Call people in your network that may know the organization and people in it. Ask about key issues and trends. Make a list of questions to ask, points to make, and STAR stories to share during your interviews.

Gather references and testimonials. Make a list of everyone who could/should be a reference for you, and then pick the two to five most relevant references for each specific opportunity you are considering. Ask permission from each reference before giving his or her name. It is even better to send a copy of your promotion, bio, and/or resume so references can give you feedback, as well as be prepared to speak about you.

Eat right, exercise, and get plenty of rest the day before the interview. If you need a haircut, get it. If you need new clothing, buy or borrow them. If your clothes need cleaning, do it. Look your best—conservatively.

Keep thinking about how you can serve with what you do best as a good steward of the grace of God.

> The good man out of the good treasure of his heart brings forth what is good; and the evil man out of the evil treasure brings forth what is evil; for his mouth speaks from that which fills his heart. Luke 6:45, NASB

PERFORM: Present yourself to the receptionist at least five minutes before the appointment. If offered something to drink, politely decline. Look around for new information on the organization, and be ready to meet the interviewer. Be especially thoughtful of and friendly to people who may not be interviewing you, but will be making observations.

Greet the interviewer with a warm smile and a firm handshake. Look them in the eyes, and tell them how glad you are to meet them. Look around the office for clues about the person like photos of family, certificates, or awards. Ask questions or comment on objects of mutual interest. When closing the interview, thank the interviewer. Say that you enjoyed the interview and learning about the company. Ask about next steps and timing, and take notes on what you find out.

PRAISE: Whether you feel the conversation went well or not, praise God from whom all blessings flow. Write thank you notes by postal and email. If you are interested in a next step, say so. If not, do not. If there is another opportunity in the same organization that appears to be a better fit, ask about it. Whatever the situation, do not burn bridges with anyone. If you are interested and do not hear back from the employer or customer by the agreed upon date, make a follow-up call and/or send an email to underscore your interest. If you hear nothing back, continue to follow-up once a week for seven weeks. If you still hear nothing, then let it go. Keep praying, networking and searching, until you get and accept the offer that's right for you.

Step 7 - Selecting

All steps connect through the first step of hearing and following the upward call of God.

Remember. You are God's. His workmanship. Created in Christ Jesus for good works. Which God prepared in advance. That you walk in them. One step at a time.

After reading through the first six steps, it's common to have thoughts about whether to stay and grow where you are, or go to another place God has appointed.

In both cases—stay or go—you are to grow from glory into glory. It is less about transition from one thing to another, and more about transformation into the image of God. Keep on keeping on in working out your salvation, continuing in sanctification and service.

As you search and sort, remember that looking for work is work. Keep seeking and seeing what God has prepared. Not only the promise of a future and a hope, but also the process of selection. Be intentional and alert as you pray for His vision, wisdom, and strength. And when it is time, trust God and take courage.

Consider yourself owned by God. He is your Employer. He is your Provider.

GET OFFERS

After interviewing for a position, don't make the mistake of passively waiting. Think and pray about how you can serve them. Find ways to follow up and demonstrate that you are prepared, passionate, and qualified. Check the news and their website to feature a different message about what they need most that you do best.

EVALUATE OFFERS

If an offer is made, listen attentively and respectfully. Take notes and repeat to verify the offer. If you are not clear about any aspect of the offer, ask questions. If it is a professional or salaried position, ask for the offer to be put in writing and sent to you. Do not immediately debate or negotiate. Do not accept or decline. Tell them how appreciative and interested you are. Ask when an answer is needed.

If you receive a written offer, review it carefully. Make a list of questions you have. If you are not good with details, ask a trusted family member or friend to review the written offer. Call or email the key contact person with questions. If you have concerns or you need to negotiate, seek to talk by phone, or even better, meet them in person.

How do you know whether a particular opportunity is really God's calling? Start by comparing the opportunity with what you learned in steps one through four. Take time away to think alone, or with your spouse, if you are married. Talk through your decision with trusted advisors, family, and close friends.

Review the 11 ways to hear and follow God's calling in step one. Do what you believe God wants you to do. If you do not feel peace inside about the decision, do not accept the offer.

MAKE OFFERS

Finally, if you don't get an offer, make an offer of your own. Think of how you can serve and offer them a one-page proposal detailing how you can meet their needs with your services for a specific period of time and cost. Also detail the results they can expect and the compensation you'd expect.

ONWARD AND UPWARD

Learning about the seven steps is usually linear, but experiencing them is always cyclical and sometimes random. Either way, the upward journey continues as you learn to love yourself correctly inward by adjusting your attitude, increasing your aptitude, and elevating your altitude. You never stop loving others compassionately by searching for ways to serve, sorting through the opportunities that arise, and selecting the good works that God has prepared for you in Christ Jesus.

We have laid out the spiritual foundations for career ministry and presented the basic building blocks of how it works. The question now is this: what will you do with them?

REFLECTION QUESTIONS

1. *How would the career ministry building block of Searching (seeking to serve) affect the other ministry areas of my church?*

2. *How would the career ministry building block of Sorting and Selecting help anyone in my church choose, not only career focus, but also ministry and volunteer focus?*

3. *What is one spiritual next step from this chapter that I can share with my church or team? What is one practical next step?*

Go

SERVANT LEADERS

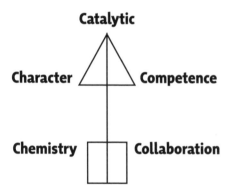

**MAKE AND EQUIP DISCIPLES
TO BE FITTED AND HELD TOGETHER**

CHAPTER 7

Make
DISCIPLES

In Parts 1 and 2 we talked about "the why and the what" of career ministry. These last three chapters are about "the how." This section will give you the tools to identify leaders, build a team, and help people follow God's calling and strengthen the Church.

> Therefore go and make disciples of all nations, baptizing them in the name of the Father and of the Son and of the Holy Spirit, and teaching them to obey everything I have commanded you. And surely I am with you always, to the very end of the age. Matthew 28:19–20

Reverend Harry Tisdale pulled up to the stop sign and held up a hand mirror to see left and right. It was the first time I noticed that he could not turn his head. He suffered crippling arthritis, which forced him to resign as rector at Holy Trinity Episcopal Parish in Decatur, GA. What a great example of a servant leader who made disciples as he fought the good fight.

Whenever a newcomer came to Holy Trinity, he visited them. He used his strengths and experience to implement his vision. He also used his weaknesses to create a church community. People saw courage, humor, and honesty that were inspiring because the arthritis was crippling his entire body. The young vibrant minister they met in the 1940s could no longer play baseball, music, or dance. His spirit in the face of the ruinous disease was a clear reminder that we are all imperfect and yet forgiven and fortified by God.

Without my even knowing it, he saved my life by modeling the life of Christ. In the midst of terrible pain, he never complained. His weakness invited others to be strong, and they accepted it with joy. While he decreased, Christ increased. He created a community of active leaders who had faith and fun. God was worshipped, and members were engaged. Not only did the church grow, but three more churches were planted. The church took on social issues such as racial integration and women's rights. Rev. Harry led with the belief that if the community was not different because of the church, then the church has no reason to be in the community.

It's not that I remember much about being taught Christian principles and practices. I think that I caught them. Right under my feet, the Lord was building a firm foundation through Rev. Harry. While I am quite sure that invitations to accept Jesus Christ as my Lord and Savior were offered, I either did not hear them or just ignored them.

When I left for college, I left behind my life in church. Hidden in my heart, however, was the first of many faithful servant leaders who saved my life. God used Rev. Harry and how he lived to start the process of making me a disciple.

> What, then, is Apollos? And what is Paul? Servants through whom you believed, even as the Lord gave opportunity to each one. I planted, Apollos watered, but God was causing the growth. So then neither the one who plants nor the one who waters is anything, but God who causes the growth. Now he who plants and he who waters are one; but each will receive his own reward according to his own labor. For we are God's fellow workers; you are God's field, God's building. 1 Corinthians 3:5-15, NASB

I have served hundreds of pastors and ministry leaders through the Crossroads Career ministry over the past 28 years, and I have come to a conclusion: they have the hardest best job in the world. Not until now have I fully appreciated who they are and what they do.

While I have also served business, church, ministry, and even government organizations as either a corporate executive or an executive search consultant, I now want to focus on what I believe is the most important position in the world.

SERVANT LEADERS IN THE CHURCH

By servant leadership, I mean you are a servant first, and then a leader second. Servant leaders shepherd others, employing their gifts, passions, and calling as good stewards of the manifold grace of God. See 1 Peter 4:10.

Servant leaders in the Church, aka the body of Christ, may be in paid or volunteer jobs in an organization. Or they may function one-on-one or as part of a team outside of an organization.

Of all the people who need a faith-based, Christ-centered approach to their work, career development, and job search, servant leaders are first.

For the purposes of this book, I would like to propose we consider servant leadership in two different but overlapping roles: pastors and ministry leaders.

PASTORS

I think of a pastor as one who has been ordained by an official religious organization and has earned a four or more year degree from a seminary or Bible college. Pastors teach and preach in churches and are authorized to conduct religious rites and ceremonies.

The word pastor is defined as "a spiritual overseer; especially a clergyman serving a local church or parish," according to Merriam-Webster. The fruit of pastoral labors in view of the gospel is often described as salvation, sanctification, and service. As ministries, those functions are called evangelism, discipleship, and care. To describe the calling of a pastor in the simplest of terms, may I propose that pastors save lives—not just eternally, but also immediately and progressively?

Thrill of victory

I love what John Piper, who served 33 years as pastor of Bethlehem Baptist Church in Minneapolis, wrote in his top 30 reasons that being a pastor is a great thing. These reasons include amazing truths such as, "The gospel is the greatest news ever sent. And pastors revel in believing it and telling it every day," and also, "Heaven is a great destiny. And pastors aim in everything to help people get there."[1]

Agony of defeat

Pastors also get an up-close-and-personal look at the hurt and dysfunction caused by sin wreaking havoc in people's lives. People look to pastors for help and comfort in the most challenging circumstances. On an almost daily basis, pastors talk with couples on the verge of divorce, with individuals in the midst of grief from the loss of a loved one, or with people generally worn down by difficult circumstances. The work can be continually demanding, just like being a shepherd constantly on duty.

Human beings are actually quite similar to sheep. First of all, they are always hungry. Secondly, they wander away following their appetites. Thirdly, they can get lost. Fourthly, sheep bite. As shepherds of people, we are surprised when people bite so we feel the pain and get mad. The natural thing is to either bite back or walk away, vowing never to feed sheep again.

Feeding sheep is a labor of love. If you get close enough to love someone, you are close enough to get hurt. Remember that while we are tending to people's felt needs and seeking to meet real needs, we will get bit.

If you are a pastor, and you smell smoke, it could be you. Burnout is more common that you might think. From health woes such as rising obesity, hypertension, and depression rates, to family and marriage concerns, being a pastor is not without major challenges.[2]

LifeWay also conducted research on pastor attitudes and found that a full 98% agree with the statement, "I feel privileged to be a pastor," with 93% strongly agreeing. Only about 0.5% of pastors disagree with the statement. Yet more than half (55%) also agree with the statement, "I find that it is easy to get discouraged," and 55% say being in pastoral ministry makes them feel lonely at times.[3]

Long hours are another issue for pastors with 65% of senior pastors saying they work 50 or more hours a week with at least 8% putting in more than 70 hours.[4] These long hours and additional pressures also take a toll on family life. Almost 10% of pastors in a LifeWay survey indicated they spend nine hours a week or fewer with family members.[5] One anecdote on Pastor Eugene Cho's blog post "Death by Ministry" even suggested that, according to life insurance companies, being a pastor was considered as dangerous and unhealthy as deep sea welding and logging![6]

Two jobs in one

Whew! Sounds challenging, and it's no wonder since pastors are doing at least two jobs in one. When I recently searched O*NET (*www.onetonline.org*), my favorite source of occupational information, the job of pastor resulted in two separate and substantial definitions.

Clergy - Conduct religious worship and perform other spiritual functions associated with beliefs and practices of religious faith or denomination. Provide spiritual and moral guidance and assistance to members.

Director of Religious Activities and Education - Plan, direct, or coordinate programs designed to promote the religious education or activities of a denominational group.

The age of specialization began in Genesis with Adam and Eve's two boys. One was a farmer and the other was a rancher. As mankind multiplied, so did the number of occupations. All the way through the Old Testament you can see a wide variety of jobs and careers. There were even ministry or spiritual jobs that became available. In fact, one of the 12 Tribes—the Levites—got pastor jobs. God had even appointed a senior pastor—Aaron. The duties of these priests were listed in Numbers 18, and included both the spiritual aspect of attending to the sanctuary, where God's presence lived on the earth, and attending to the practical matters of the tent as priests. Some priests were dedicated to working "inside the veil," attending to the altar, while others were dedicated to the matters of the outer courts of the tent: keeping the furnishings clean and in order, attending to ritual sacrifices, etc. This delineation was so important that God warned anyone who came within the veil without the proper credentials would be put to death. Yikes!

Today, it is ever more specialized and complex. I pulled up the jobs site *Simply-Hired.com* and entered the keyword "pastor." In the United States alone, there were 8,765 pastor jobs listed. See for yourself. Pastor jobs come in a variety of sizes and shapes: senior, executive, evangelism, discipleship, teaching, education, connections, assimilation, community, outreach, worship, pastoral, care, campus, counseling, stewardship, men's, women's, college, youth, children, chaplain, and more.

MINISTRY LEADERS

Partnered with pastors in the work of the Church are ministry leaders from the congregation and community.

For example, in my church, the average weekend attendance is 2,500. With only four pastors, were it not for ministry leaders from the congregation, our flock would go hungry and get lost.

Pastors are ministry leaders, of course, focusing on "clergy duties" and equipping others for spiritual leadership, such as elders, deacons, overseers, and directors of activities and education for evangelism, discipleship, and care, as well as the business of the Church. Here is how the Apostle Paul described this leadership development process:

> So Christ himself gave the apostles, the prophets, the evangelists, the pastors and teachers, to equip his people for works of service, so that the body of Christ may be built up. Ephesians 4:11–12

The pastors and servant leaders in our church are also partnered with ministry leaders in the community from a chaplain in a nearby prison and a director of a county food pantry to missionaries and ministries around the world.

Beyond organizational considerations are the even more important functions of living in Christ in the process of salvation, sanctification, and service. As we are on the way, I think all servant leaders need to be prayerful, intentional, alert, and equipped to respond to felt needs for family, friends, health, wealth, and work.

TRENDS IN THE CHURCH

Change is constant. Whether it will be for the best or the worst remains to be seen, but emerging trends will change the face of pastoral roles and ministry leader engagement.

LifeWay Christian Resources president and CEO Thom Rainer identified several examples of future trends, such as the consolidation of smaller churches, the rise of mega- and multi-site churches, and the larger demand for bi-vocational pastors. In addition, he says more churches will partner with seminaries to apprentice future pastors and denominations will continue their trend in reducing involvement in pastoral selection.[7]

After reading through details and trends of being a pastor or ministry leader, you might be overwhelmed or under-inspired. You may even feel confused, or perhaps misemployed or misplaced.

The main reason is that most people, including servant leaders in the Church, start by looking for a position or developing a career. Putting your ambitions ahead of God's calling is putting the cart before the horse. You will never be the right person in the right place until you put God in the center of your life.

WHAT'S NEXT FOR YOU?

As a servant leader shepherding a flock, it's important to know where you're going so that the sheep know where to go. **So where are you going? I mean this question personally—what's on the horizon for you?** Have you considered where God is calling you, or have you just gotten stuck in the day-to-day, run-of-the-mill operations of keeping your church going.

It's easy to believe that once you become a church leader, it's all you'll do until you die, but the reality is that we all have an expiration date. You only have so many miles you can go, only so many sermons you can preach. And the flock you're leading is looking for you to have a legacy plan so that when the shepherd moves on, the sheep don't scatter. Perhaps you've had a clear understanding of your calling, but you've never really thought about it in terms of a career.

Everyone needs career ministry, including you. Are you hearing God's upward calling step by step? If you are, you're putting yourself and your congregation in an excellent posture for a bright and hope-filled future. When you put yourself on the path of finding a career within your calling, you'll find you're far better equipped to offer Christ-centered, whole-life ministry to those you lead.

REFLECTION QUESTIONS

1. *Why did I decide to become a pastor or ministry leader? What's the purpose of the work I do?*

2. *What are some emotions that describe the work that I do?*

3. *What are one spiritual and one practical next step from this chapter that I can share with my church or team?*

CHAPTER 8

Fitted
AND HELD TOGETHER

How would you like to read as a pastor or write as a ministry leader a note like this one by Jim Carow, who leads the iWorks career ministry at Idlewild Church near Tampa, Florida:

> "I don't know where to begin about iWork tonight.
>
> Do I start with Derica, one of our volunteers who celebrated by bringing a cake and told of how she did not settle for less when God had the best out there for her?
>
> Maybe I should start with Rick's devotion where he mentioned that Frank Lloyd Wright was still designing buildings at age 92 because he kept his mind, body, soul, and spirit fit.
>
> Or do I start with our 'buffet/smorgasbord/helpdesk' approach tonight which was wildly popular where all 40 people in the room got to be in instructional groups no larger than 4.
>
> They each got to spend 35 minutes with 5 different instructors on 5 different topics. It was a high energy, great learning session.
>
> Or should I tell of Tomas who drove over from Orlando at the pastor's wife's urging. Tomas has $75 in his wallet for gas and no other money. He shared his testimony with me, which included lots of struggles. My prayer for him is that he can focus on that one thing that he can do. Right now he is all over the place.
>
> Or maybe it is my neighbor, Jane, who once proudly declared she is an "agnostic" and now has been to iWork twice and is participating in our prayer requests.

Maybe I should tell about Joe, who graduated three years ago, bringing a neighbor who admitted he had a terrible attitude, and now is ready to do something positive.

Should I start with our ten volunteers who did such a great job of teaching tonight?

I think I will go with "God was glorified tonight."

Pretty exciting report, isn't it? How would you like to read one every week? Jim's pastors do. That's because Jim has a servant's view of leadership and teamwork.

PICK A LEADER

Do you start with the leader first who builds a team? Maybe it is better to recruit people to a team, and then see who among them might rise to be the leader?

I have done both successfully, but most times the leader is picked first. If two or more step forward with interest to start a ministry, look for the one who naturally begins to plan, organize, direct, and follow up with the rest. **It is usually best to pick the person who is skilled at leading versus the one who may know the most about job search or career development.** Great subject matter experts are not always the best at leading.

May I recommend for your consideration five characteristics to seek and develop in servant leaders – be they pastors or ministry leaders? They are...

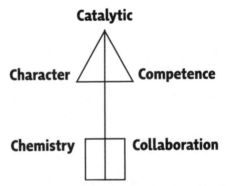

I have been using the first three for many years as personal leadership dynamics to recruit and develop the right leaders in the right roles in serving church and ministry clients as well as business and government organizations. I learned to use all five characteristics from my pastor at Transformation Church as it has grown from 176 people at its first service in 2010 to over 2,500 average weekly attendance now in 2015.

PERSONAL LEADERSHIP DYNAMICS

Twenty-five years ago I started my own five-year study of leaders and leadership as I struggled to keep up with the growth of my executive search firm. I learned the most from one book that is still being updated, published, and used today: *The Leadership Challenge* by James M. Kouzes and Barry Posner.

I still have my original copy all marked up, including page 22 where I underlined three criteria of a study about how employees perceived their top management: Trustworthiness, Expertise, and Dynamism. In the margin I wrote: "TED – the perfect leader."[1]

Today I still teach an enhanced version of the same model of personal leadership dynamics, translating TED into the 3Cs: Character, Competence and Catalytic.

Let me share an outline of the three characteristics and the ten behaviors that I believe are always required for leadership regardless of the role. This is especially critical when leading a career ministry team in a church, the members of which are volunteering their time and talents.

Character

Meet commitments:	Be a promise keeper
Walk with integrity:	Be consistent in words-deeds
Serve sincerely:	Support, care, and trust

Would you follow someone who you did not trust? If a leader breaks promises, says one thing but does another, or seems not to be interested in the well being of others, how long will it take followers to stop following?

Competence

Know thy stuff:	Be expert in your craft
Manage things:	Plan, organize, follow-up
Direct people:	Recruit, train, assign

Can you follow leaders who do not know what they are doing? If they do not plan or are not organized, how do you know what you are supposed to do? If they cannot get the right people in the right roles, how confusing is that going to be?

Catalytic

Vision:	See a preferred future
Wisdom:	Know how to get there
Strength:	Build energy and resources
Courage:	Has guts to step up and out

Have you met people with character who are competent and yet you cannot follow because they are not going anywhere? Or maybe they cast vision, but don't know how to execute or they cannot get the resources needed? Finally, if they don't have the courage to move forward, how can you?

All three characteristics are required to encourage and stimulate others to follow you be it one-on-one, in teams, or in organizations. While I believe being catalytic gets most of the attention in leadership literature, it is character and competence that attract and assure people. A serious deficit in any one of these three characteristics, however, raises barriers in your leadership ability.

For large teams and organizations, something more than character, competence, and catalytic is required.

TEAM WORKS

Teamwork makes the dream work. My favorite teamwork verse in the Bible is:

> But speaking the truth in love, we are to grow up in all aspects into Him who is the head, even Christ, from whom the whole body, being fitted and held together by what every joint supplies, according to the proper working of each individual part, causes the growth of the body for the building up of itself in love. Ephesians 4:15-16, NASB

Every team needs its own mix of different members based on the six factors of what each person does best. Here's a quick list from Chapter 5 about Step 3 Aptitude:

1. **Experiences:** *Your background - personal, educational, vocational*

2. **Abilities:** *What you do best - talents, knowledge, skills*

3. **Personality:** *How you do best what you do best - natural behaviors*

4. **Interests:** *What you like best - people, places, things, activities you enjoy*

5. **Values:** *What is important—your work and life purpose and principles*

6. **Factor X:** *The presence and power of the Holy Spirit, who manifests spiritual gifts and calling.*

Just as each person is a unique mix of these factors, each team is a mix of servant leaders who come together for the work of ministry. Usually there is common unity among members as it relates to interests and values. Diversity is usually important as it relates to different experiences, abilities, and personality traits needed.

For career ministries to start and grow, two additional servant leadership characteristics are required to be fitted and held together:

Chemistry
A team with chemistry is built on positive relationships. Members smile a lot and like each other. They know about and care for one another. Oh yeah, and they win a lot, too.

Chemistry happens when a unique relational mix of diverse backgrounds, personalities, work styles, values, and interests come together for a common purpose. It has an elusive quality that isn't always easy to define, but you can tell when it is missing.

Let me describe what I mean from the ministry side of my life.

The career team at my church started with two members who knew and liked each other, were very different from one another, and were committed to the same vision. Three years later there are 18 members including the original two who share leadership of the team, nine who are core teammates, five who come occasionally when asked and available, plus two church staff members who support the rest of the career team along with another 10 ministries.

Becoming part of the team includes completing a ministry interest survey, interviewing with at least two of the core team, background investigation and a confidentiality agreement. New members start by serving alongside core teammates, usually in hospitality and admin roles, not only to learn ministry functions, but especially to build relationships. Training and equipping includes two half-day workshops teaching the 7-step career ministry process using our

workbook and online career ministry resources. We stay in continuous communication with one another by phone, email, the church intranet system, team
projects, and social times together – typically with food.

All of us pay attention to one another to discover what each teammate does
best and who needs it most. Not only do we seek good chemistry through relationships but also collaboration.

Collaboration
Co-laboring is the functional side of teamwork. It involves planning and organizing supported by processes and systems. On our ministry team there are
two co-leaders who take turns being the point person. They support three core
teammates, each one responsible for a different ministry environment – quarterly workshops, weekly support groups, and ongoing individual coaching.

Each person has their unique role to fill, and by working together, everyone
achieves greater goals than working alone. **It's not just many hands make work
light, but rather the right hands in the right places make work good.**

CALLED TO LEADERSHIP
Consider a cupbearer named Nehemiah, for example. How likely a candidate
would he be to leave his job in the king's palace? Yet, he responded when he
heard of the distress and reproach of his people and the broken down walls of
Jerusalem...

> **"When I heard these words, I sat down and wept and mourned for days;
> and I was fasting and praying before the God of heaven." Nehemiah 1:4,
> NASB**

Jerusalem mattered to him. So he prayed for God to remember his loving kind-
ness. Then he continued his job, prepared a plan, and waited. The king noticed
something was not right with Nehemiah, and asked him, "Why the long face?"

Nehemiah is suddenly faced with a crossroads in his career: does he risk sharing
with the king the deep desire in his heart to lead the effort to restore his home-
land? Or does he keep his head down and continue with business as usual? It
wasn't an easy decision—we know because the text says that at this moment
he was "very much afraid."

His response is full of leadership lessons. He chooses to tell the king what's
bothering him. In spite of his fear, he stepped up and stepped out. When the
king asked what he needed, Nehemiah prayed on the spot while he was pre-
senting the plan. His impromptu plan to restore Jerusalem was immediately ap-
proved by the king, not because of Nehemiah's brilliance, but in his own words,
"because the good hand of my God was upon me."

When you are called to leadership, what is your first response? I remember when one of my clients—a large corporation division president—asked if I would consider leading human resources. I quickly said "Thank you, but no." Without really thinking about it, I had shot his request out of the sky like it was skeet. Later that day I was praying and told God what had happened. I felt like God responded, "Why did you not ask Me first?" Oops! I went back to my client, apologized and applied for the job. A month later, my client and I concluded my leading human resources would not be a good assignment. But the result was an even better relationship with my client and a greater ability to serve him as a consultant.

When you think God is calling you, answer Him. **Always take every thought captive in obedience to Christ,** especially if He might be calling you to a specific leadership role.

New ministries will naturally have a surge of momentum when they first get started, and that makes leaders feel really good. But it's almost inevitable that the excitement will wear off, momentum will dwindle, and then leaders will have second thoughts. *Is this really a good idea? Are we being effective at all? Should we just call it quits?* Leaders persevere through these quitting points and do what it takes to create new momentum. They continue to cast vision. They continue to pray, prep, perform, and praise. And most of all, they face their fears and lean into problems with faith and trust in God. They do this for the sake of the people they're called to serve.

In the last chapter we will take a look at the steps to setting up a career ministry in your church or organization. Let's go!

REFLECTION QUESTIONS

1. *What role can I play in starting or growing a career ministry?*

2. *Who should be on the career team in my church or ministry? How can the team members be fitted and held together?*

3. *Who might be the best leader for career ministry? What can I do to find him or her?*

CHAPTER 9

Equip
THE SAINTS

Do you remember the story Jesus told in response to a question about "who is my neighbor?"

> Jesus replied and said, "A man was going down from Jerusalem to Jericho, and fell among robbers, and they stripped him and beat him, and went away leaving him half dead." And by chance a priest was going down on that road, and when he saw him, he passed by on the other side. Likewise a Levite also, when he came to the place and saw him, passed by on the other side. But a Samaritan, who was on a journey, came upon him and when he saw him, he felt compassion, and came to him and bandaged up his wounds, pouring oil and wine on them; and he put him on his own beast, and brought him to an inn and took care of him. On the next day he took out two denarii and gave them to the innkeeper and said, "Take care of him; and whatever more you spend, when I return I will repay you."
>
> "Which of these three do you think proved to be a neighbor to the man who fell into the robbers' hands?"
>
> And he said, "The one who showed mercy toward him." Then Jesus said to him, "Go and do the same." Luke 10:30-37, NASB

Given the number of neighbors in your congregation and community who lost jobs, hate jobs or want God's calling, the prospect of starting and growing a career ministry may seem overwhelming.

How do you find and equip saints for the work of service? Help is closer than you might think.

Start a career ministry

Join our national network of churches, community groups, schools and professional affiliates.

I invite you to connect with Crossroads Career Network, a national membership of churches and ministries equipped to help people find jobs, careers, and God's calling. Go to *www.CrossroadsCareer.org* and click the church icon under "Start a Career Ministry" to see a resource list, connect to member services, and register to join.

Pray for God to raise up servant leaders from your congregation. Consider the five characteristics of leaders that we just looked at in Chapter 8. Often the best choice is someone who is already unofficially helping people to find jobs, develop their careers, or discover God's calling. It could be someone with work experience in human resources, recruiting, career development, or coaching. Perhaps they have management experience that includes hiring and placing employees. It is very likely that they would have walked through their own career crossing. They understand and appreciate God's provision personally.

Pray, too, for a staff member who wants to support such a ministry. This can be a big key to success since a staff member often has tighter communication with church leaders and a greater understanding of available resources and how to appropriately and effectively use them for the ministry.

CASTING VISION

A vision of the future will transform how you live today.[1] As you raise up a team, you'll find that your primary function is casting vision. And then casting it again. And then casting it again. Vision leaks, and without vision, the effort will flounder, and the leaders you're trying to focus toward a goal will cast off restraint.

How do you begin casting the vision? A good place to start is by buying four more copies of this book. Be ready to give this book to prospective team leaders and supporting staff members. Pick a date by which you'd like them to read it, then schedule some time to discuss it. It is important to get everyone on the same page.

Start asking your church staff and lay leaders about who in the church is helping others with job, career, and calling-related issues. Be alert for whomever God brings, so long as they are a sincere follower of Jesus.

TEAM ROLES

There are three basic ministry functions that must be prepared, so you'll want to look for individuals capable of serving in the following three areas:

1. **Leading:** *Vision casting, recruiting, planning, organizing, directing, and following up*

2. **Ministering:** *Helping people find jobs, careers, and God's calling*

3. **Supporting:** *Praying, promoting, and coordinating administrative tasks*

Sometimes one leader is good at two of these functions, which is a bonus, but it's rare that just one person can do all three. This is a good thing, because ministry is always best done as a team.

As the leadership team begins taking shape, use a five-stage process of praying, preparing, performing, promoting and praising that surrounds and supports all the people involved in and touched by the ministry. In building the career ministry, these five things will also be geared toward making beneficial connections and building the relationships that will make this ministry successful in your congregation.

IN EVERYTHING BY PRAYER

Through prayer we have direct communication with our Heavenly Father. As we pray, we show our dependence on and trust in Him. Successful career ministries start, grow, and renew by prayer being first and throughout. One of our member churches calls prayer the "engine room" of its ministries.

Prayer powers and protects ministry. Continually invite everyone on the career ministry team to pray, not only for people to whom they are ministering, but also for one another, the ministry, church, and community.

One of the first prayers is to ask for more prayer warriors and a chief to lead them. If your church has a prayer ministry, ask if they would be willing to pray for requests received through the career ministry. Perhaps someone on the prayer team would also be interested in being on the career ministry team to coordinate prayer requests with praying warriors. Always be on the lookout for people who love to pray every day, wherever they are in the church. Nothing is more important than prayer.

> The weapons we fight with are not the weapons of the world. On the
> contrary, they have divine power to demolish strongholds. We demolish
> arguments and every pretension that sets itself up against the knowledge of
> God, and we take captive every thought to make it obedient to Christ.
> 2 Corinthians 10:4–5

Provide confidential prayer request forms at all events and meetings to make it easy for everyone to make their needs known. It is not hard to imagine that the enemy has a major share of our economy and employment. Think of prayer as an offensive weapon, so we ask you to consider praying at four levels...

1. Pray for people who are ministry leaders, supporting pastors, team members, and career explorers. Pray for their protection and provision. Ask God to guard them and guide them. Ask everyone for confidential prayer requests about all things important to them, not just in career ministry, but also in their personal and professional lives. When someone asks for prayer, pray for that person immediately, as well as during your planned prayer time.

2. Pray for plans, both preparation and its performance. Ask God for His spirit of wisdom and revelation. Remember the saying, "Work as if it all depends

on you. Pray as if it all depends on God." Pray before, during, and after career meetings and events. Successful career ministries in the Crossroads Career Network consistently report that prayer is the number one reason for success.

3. Pray for your church. Not just the career ministry, but the whole ministry of the church. Pray specifically for pastors, staff, and leaders. Be proactive and ask for requests from them, especially those with whom you work in the church.

4. Pray for your community. A recent survey revealed 62% of the churches reported people from the community asking for help with unemployment. Many of our churches report that most of the people who come to their career groups and events are not from their church, but rather from the community. Pray not only for career explorers, but also employers and other churches.[2]

PREPARE

As you are praying, make lists of needs, resources, and people. As you begin to match resources with needs, continue praying about where the career ministry best fits organizationally in your church. Churches organize their ministries in a variety of ways, and it's important to make it a good fit with your leadership, structure, and culture.

The resources you have will help determine how the ministry will take shape in your church. Your primary resources are people, time, and money.

1. **People:** You are looking for two key people: the ministry leader (usually a volunteer leader in the congregation) and a supporting staff member or pastor. Be on alert for which pastors, staff members, or church leaders are most interested in, or perhaps called to, work with the career ministry.

   The role of the career ministry leader is to plan, organize, direct, and evaluate the activities of the ministry. They'll be the spokesperson representing the career ministry to others. Most importantly, they'll be leading the effort by seeking to serve others in your congregation and in your community.

   The role of the supporting staff member is to advise and support the club and the ministry leader. They can help provide rooms and resources to the group, as well as help integrate with other ministries. They'll also act as an advocate representing the group to the overall organization, but especially to church leadership and the board.

2. **Time:** You can begin the ministry any time during the year. Many churches like to start new programs either in January, June, or September. We recommend a three-month planning schedule in order to coordinate with other activities and facility use, as well as provide enough time to survey needs and resources, plan and organize, and recruit volunteers and explorers.

3. **Money:** As part of your plan, you will need to consider costs and a budget for your ministry. The annual membership in the Crossroads Career Network includes full access to all career and ministry resources available online, and for some churches, that is all that is needed.

PERFORM

One of the great things about career ministry is how flexible and scalable it is. It can take place one-on-one, in small groups, or even in larger seminars. It can happen in person, over the phone, or via email. You'll need to sort through all the available options and decide what environments best fit your church for the ministry.

Ministering environments are models or formats for ministry through which the team creates time, space, and activity. Each environment reaches out, engages, and serves different groups with different needs for different purposes. Most churches start with one or maybe two environments, and then grow and change as need or opportunity provides.

The Crossroads Career 7-Step Process and Work Book provide a common framework and curriculum with freedom to meet people's needs. You can get a copy at *www.CrossroadsCareer.org/store*.

Below is a list of different ministry models from which you can select or mix and match:

HIGH ENGAGEMENT MINISTRY MODELS

Coaching individuals through the process of job search is especially helpful as a complement to benevolence and financial assistance ministries. People with money problems are often unemployed or underemployed, so that help with generating income is equally as important as budgeting and debt reduction. One-to-one coaching is also appropriate for executives and entrepreneurs who prefer individual and confidential help in dealing with issues at work. We also find as needed individual coaching is a good complement to our other ministry environments, especially support groups and study groups/classes. The Work Book is used in all cases as a reference guide to keep discussions on track.

Support groups are primarily relationship environments where everyone quickly learns how to pray, support, network, and share ideas. These are facilitated weekly meetings that begin with reviewing and celebrating positives from the past week and finish with each person sharing their goals and the help they need for the coming week. It is a flexible environment focused on transforming a lonely journey into a place where job seekers and career explorers help each another throughout every week. Again, the Work Book can be used as a quick reference guide in every meeting.

Study groups and classes provide a powerful combination of small group dynamics and instructions with exercises using the 7-step process. Each group or class environment is led by one or more experienced team members that facilitate using the Work Book as the core curriculum. It was originally designed as an eight-week course of two hours per session. Teams have successfully modified the curriculum for unemployed participants as a two-and-half week, seven-session crash course. Other teams have lengthened it to 13 weeks for people who are interested in career development and discovering their calling.

COMMUNITY OUTREACH MINISTRY MODELS

Workshops or seminars meet the career/job search training needs of many people. You can choose one-hour to full-day formats, either focusing on specific job search topics like resumes, networking, and interviews, or teaching the whole 7-step process. A half-day/four-hour format is a great way to introduce your new group, as well as a popular community outreach.

Network meetings: Regularly scheduled network meeting events can be a great outreach to the community. They include a featured speaker on some aspect of faith-based job or career development, plus facilitated networking time, usually offered in a two-hour format.

Job connections: There are three ways to provide job connections with employers for job seekers and career explorers. The Crossroads Career website includes free access to over 100,000 fresh job listings and resume postings that are searchable by over 1,000 registered employers. Career fairs featuring employers with available jobs can be done with local labor department career centers and directly with employers themselves. Employers can register for posting jobs and searching resumes at *www.CrossroadsCareer. org* and clicking on the employer icon...

Are you an employer?

Looking for quality candidates? Sign-up to post jobs, search resumes and connect with our network.

SPECIAL FOCUS MINISTRY MODELS

High school teens: At my church we completed our first teen workshop series teaching students and their parents about career, calling, college, and finances. We learned how poorly equipped parents and their teens are to prepare for life after high school. As part of our Teens-to-Careers program development, we have developed a basic faith-based curriculum that can be used in church youth groups and Christian high schools.

College students: Having worked with students and faculty at five different colleges and universities, I learned that career services are often under-resourced and that students graduate ill prepared to find a job, let alone think about God's calling in their future career. Crossroads Career Network has developed and continues to beta test Teens-to-Careers programs based on the 7-step process, but tailored to the needs of youth coming from high school, as well as to adults returning for further education or new career direction. There are also excellent resources for college career services as well as curriculum for youth groups and college-age ministries.

Retiring seniors: An increasing number of seniors are coming to career ministries for help. Fifty-four percent of senior workers say they'll work after retiring from their current career – up from 45% last year.[3] Of this group, 81% say they'll most likely work part-time, while 19% plan to continue working full-time.[4] Instead of just retiring, I am teaching seniors whether they need to work or not about "re-higher-meant" based on their gifts, passions, and calling!

Prison ministry: My church has four campuses, two of which are in men's prisons. Our career ministry team has begun teaching prison inmate leaders the 7-step process and building a job readiness program to help men successfully transition from prison to society. It is a big need and opportunity. According to the U.S. Bureau of Justice Statistics 2,266,800 adults were incarcerated in U.S. federal and state prisons and county jails at year-end 2011 – about 0.94% of adults in the U.S. resident population.[5] One study tracked 404,638 prisoners in 30 states after their release from prison in 2005. The researchers found that within three years of release, about two-thirds (67.8%) of released prisoners were rearrested.[6]

SUMMING UP

Regardless of the ministry environment used or the group you are trying to reach, the core 7-step process works in the hands of called and equipped servant leaders.

Our strategy is to bring the best of high-tech and high-touch together. Everything online is for you to minister on-the-ground, helping people to not only find jobs and careers, but most especially hear and follow God's calling one step at a time.

PROMOTE YOUR MINISTRY

Promotion is about praising and proclaiming God's promises, provision, and power—past, present, and future. It is born out of prayer, seeking, and sharing His message for each ministering environment offered.

Men shall speak of the power of Your awesome acts, and I will tell of Your greatness. Psalm 145:6, NASB

Leverage the power of story. As a career ministry, you have the unique opportunity to reach a large group of people. One of the most effective ways to promote your services and events is by telling others what you have seen the Lord do. That's why we are all here—to see God move.

Hearing stories from others who have overcome their job crisis or found their calling by God's faithful leading allows people walking through similar challenges to know that they can also emerge in a better place than where they started. Even people who don't believe in Christ will find hope in simple stories of people using the practical skills they learned at your event to land a job. And when we meet the physical needs of people, it provides the Holy Spirit access to the door of their hearts.

It is really about promoting the work of the Lord, and when we do this, promoting career ministry events will fall into place.

The most effective form of promotion is via grassroots efforts. Share personal invitations with family, friends, schoolmates, workmates, neighbors, and church members. Wherever you go, whoever you meet, invite anyone who says anything about being unemployed, seeking a job, needing a new career, or wanting to hear God's calling.

Carry ministry cards with you that have your contact and event information to hand out. Print cards for everyone on your team so everybody is prepared to share. You can also give cards to pastors, staff members, and leaders in the church, and make sure to equip them with as much information about career ministry as possible.

Ask for referrals, especially from ministry leaders in prayer, care, benevolence, financial stewardship, and small groups. Present what you are doing and how you can help other ministries. Use all the usual church communication tools, such as bulletins, slides, newsletters, and websites.

I recommend that one person be responsible for coordinating promotion to attract explorers, employers, and potential team members to connect with your career ministry and online resources. Having one person oversee the promotion of the ministry will help ensure that the details are completed and will help distribute the work behind the scenes. That person could already be on your communications team as a staff member or volunteer. Or you might find a pro-motion coordinator interested in the career team—perhaps even going through their own career crossroads and needing help.

PRAISE

As a child and a teen I praised God every Sunday at Holy Trinity Episcopal Par-ish, just outside the Atlanta city limits. I can still see in my mind's eye Reverend Tisdale in white robes, arms outstretched, leading us in songs and hymns and spiritual songs. I can still hear in my heart his leading us through Doxology.

If we did not sing robustly enough, the good reverend would have us sing again with more vim and vigor. Oh, how much I appreciate his love for the Lord, his genuine praise. Even now, I smile with welling tears in my eyes that he cared enough to make us sing praises to our utmost for God's highest.

I had that same feeling the other night after coaching a couple of single women struggling in their current jobs and seeking the Lord and His calling. While the two hours together were in the nits and grits of writing better resumes, we explored how God had made each of them His masterpieces. As they were leav-ing, they were following God. After they left, I praised God for His generous gift of my seeing into their hearts and sowing seeds of truth and hope. I was physi-cally and mentally exhausted, but I was spiritually soaring.

When God finished each day of His work of creating heaven and earth, He saw it was good. After a week of work, and His work was finished...

> God saw all that He had made, and behold, it was very good.
> Genesis 1:31, NASB

I think God was so pleased that He took the seventh day off to celebrate, to enjoy the fruit of His works, and to rest. I don't think He rested because He was tired, but because He wanted to enjoy what had been accomplished.

Now He works in and through you and me by the enabling power of His Holy Spirit. What an awesome privilege and honor that we can be co-laborers with the Creator of the created. How can we not celebrate, appreciate, and communi-cate with Him Who made all? Not only can we and should we praise and glorify God alone, but also do so before others...

> Let your light shine before men in such a way that they may see your good works, and glorify your Father who is in heaven. Matthew 5:16, NASB

As you complete each step of leading, ministering, and supporting, pause to praise God from Whom all blessings flow. Be a good steward of the ministry by gathering and sharing stories of what God is doing in people's lives. Testimonies should be a part of almost any gathering—especially gatherings of leaders and volunteers. Celebrate every job found, every promotion, every interview.

Keep statistics of how many people are served, and spread the good news with the team and pastors about what's happening. Measuring results helps you not only see what to celebrate, but also where you can improve. It's even a good idea to survey explorers after courses and workshops.

Let me share two emails I received together from a ministry leader that illustrate not only what God is doing in the midst of job search, but also the praise and thanksgiving being shared by ministry team members:

Jobseeker: "It has been such a pleasure meeting our group and learning from both of you and the other presenters. After each meeting I came home excited and happy to share with my family. I am excited to tell you I accepted an offer and will be starting my new career as a recruiter on Monday! I have no doubt it was the confidence and renewed faith and energy that helped me land this role."

Ministry Team Member: "If you only knew what I know how this woman struggled for the past several years with rejection after rejection in seeking her career path as she shared with me last week after class for at least a half hour. 'WOW' is not a big enough word here. The only appropriate response is 'Praise God!'"

OPPORTUNITY AT CROSSROADS

The intersection of jobs and Jesus in America is a very busy place. Of the 318 million people in our country, 157 million are workers passing through crossroads in their careers.[6] That means half the people you know could benefit from career ministry. Half of your community. Half of your neighbors. Half of your congregation.

Career crossroads, where crucial decisions must be made that have far-reaching consequences, is a prime place to evangelize, disciple, and care for people.

What we often don't realize on this journey is that there are crossroads made by the shadow of cross of Christ being laid across our path, so that you'll look up and see Him.

Most people arrive at a crossroads in their careers alone. It seems like hitchhiking to be standing there with your thumb out, hoping someone will stop and offer a lift. Hundreds of cars pass. You try waving, smiling, sometimes praying. Stop! Somebody please stop and give me a ride.

How great would it be to have a third person at the crossroads—someone who is equipped, who has a map, someone who can give you directions to the next place? Someone to pray with you? Someone who can cheer you on and encourage you to keep going?

This is what the Lord says:

> Stand at the crossroads and look; ask for the ancient paths, ask where the good way is, and walk in it, and you will find rest for your souls. But you said, "We will not walk in it." Jeremiah 6:16

I often measure the importance of a message by who is speaking. In this case, the speaker is the Lord God Almighty, maker of heaven and earth!

Pay attention to the four key verbs that God uses.

Stand at the crossroads, as opposed to run away or run through. Most people I know feel like taking flight or they get ready to fight.

Look before you leap. Take a good look, not just a glance and then dash. Circumspectly see every one of the 360 degrees around you. What are the circumstances surrounding you? Who is there? What are they doing? Where are road options, and where do they appear to be going?

Ask your close friends and experts. Ask about tried and true ways that have worked for them. Ask the Lord who made you and saved you. Ask where the good way is. When you ask, don't just listen, but hear. For most of us, it is even better to take notes.

Walk when you hear and see the good way. Do not delay when you hear Him say, "This is it. Move out now."

Did you notice that our key verse concluded with...

> "But you said, 'We will not walk in it.'"

It is hard to imagine why in the world someone would say no to the one true God who made the universe. We all know that Father knows best—right? But when God is talking to us, we think our situation is different. We start with the deadly phrase, "Yeah, but... " Then we start explaining why we cannot, we will not, follow Him. Do we think it is advice, or do we miss the fact that He is God who has prepared everything, including our next step?

NOW IT'S YOUR TURN

What is God calling you to do now? If you've been breezing through this book for information, great. But I'm asking you take a pause, put this book down, and pray. Stand at the crossroads. Listen for the Lord's guidance.

Career ministry connects our greatest felt need with the deepest need of our soul. People like to talk about the "high stakes" world of business, or politics, or even sports. But when it comes down to it, the Church is working in the arena with the highest stakes of all, because we're dealing with people's eternal destinies. But great rewards require great risks, and often, great sacrifice.

I believe that if you've read this book carefully, you've most likely heard God speaking to you about taking a risk, stepping out, and putting your shoulder to the plow of serving people in a greater measure. In saying yes to this call, you're in good company. Jesus Himself led the way in saying yes to the call of the Father by giving Himself to serve us, His children. He did so because He knew it would not only save us, but also allow us to live life more abundantly, to discover the good works He prepared for us. Will you partner with Him? Will you respond to the call? The choice is yours.

REFLECTION QUESTIONS

1. *Who in my church is currently equipped to help lead and disciple a career ministry? What makes them the best choice?*

2. *How can I refocus and/or consolidate other ministries in the church to align with a career ministry?*

3. *What is my next step in moving forward? What is holding me back?*

Contact Crossroads Career Network in three ways:

support@CrossroadsCareer.org
www.CrossroadsCareer.org
800-941-3566

ENDNOTES

INTRODUCTION

1. Jim Clifton, *The Coming Jobs War* (New York: Gallup, Inc, 2011).

2. George Barna, "The Economy's Impact on Churches, Part 2 of 3," https://www.barna.org/barna-update/congregations/334-the-economys-impact-on-churches-part-2-of-3-how-churches-have-adapted#.U7r_tahZt9k.

3. Ibid.

4. Tim Keller, *Every Good Endeavor: Connecting Your Work to God's Work* (New York: Dutton, 2012).

5. Amy Sherman, *Kingdom Calling: Vocational Stewardship for the Common Good* (Downers Grove, Ill., IVP Books, 2011), 20.

6. Ibid, 23.

CHAPTER 1

1. Jim Clifton, *The Coming Jobs War* (New York: Gallup, Inc, 2011).

2. Michael Michelsen, Jr., "Career Counseling" *Christianity Today* 53:8 (2009): 38.

3. Arthur Delaney, "Joblessness and Hopelessness: The Link Between Unemployment and Suicide," *Huffington Post*, New York Times, April 15, 2011. http://www.huffingtonpost.com/2011/04/15/unemployment-and-suicide_n_849428.html.

4. Ibid.

5. Dr. Rebecca Ray, Thomas Rizzacasa, and Dr. Gad Levanon, "Job Satisfaction:2013 Edition," The Conference Board, June 2013.

6. "Women at Work " Bureau of Labor Statistics, http://www.bls.gov/spotlight/2011/women/.

7. "Quick Stats on Women Workers 2010" Department of Labor, http://www.dol.gov/wb/factsheets/QS-women-work2010.htm.

8. State of the American Workplace: Employment Engagement Insights for U.S. Business Leaders, Gallup, Inc., http://www.gallup.com/services/178514/state-american-workplace.aspx.

9. Barbara Rarden, *Employed for Life*, (Knoxville: Crown Financial Ministries, 2011).

10. Johnny Cash, "No Earthly Good," *The Rambler*, Columbia Records, 1977.

11. George Barna, *Growing True Disciples: New Strategies for Producing Genuine Followers of Christ* (Colorado Springs: Waterbrook Press, 2001).

CHAPTER 2

1. Derwin Gray. *Limitless Life: You Are More Than Your Past When God Holds Your Future.* (Nashville: Thomas Nelson, 2013), 144-145.

2. Steve Crabtree, "In U.S., Depression Rates Higher for Long-Term Unemployed" *Gallup.com*, June 9, 2014, http://www.gallup.com/poll/171044/depression-rates-higher-among-long-term-unemployed.aspx.

3. Nik Wallenda, *Balance: A Story of Faith, Family, and Life on the Line* (Nashville: FaithWords, 2013).

CHAPTER 3

1. Gary O'Malley, *Life Purpose in a Nutshell: A Biblical Approach to Life Purpose and Discovery*, 1998.

2. Roger Gum, *Financial Faithfulness: Unlocking Scripture to Avoid the Distraction of Money* (Westbow Press, 2013).

CHAPTER 4

1. Oz Guinness, *The Call: Finding and Fulfilling the Central Purpose of Your Life* (Nashville: Thomas Nelson, 2003).

CHAPTER 5

1. Robert J. Kriegel and Louis Palter, *If It Ain't Broke, Break It! And Other Unconventional Wisdom for a Changing Business World* (Business Plus, 1992).

2. Ken Boa, *Face to Face: Praying the Scriptures for Intimate Worship* (Zondervan, 1997).

3. Dan Witters, Jim Asplund, and Jim Harter, "Half in U.S. Don't Use Their Strengths Throughout the Day" Gallup.com, September 12, 2012.

CHAPTER 6

1. The ideas of "WoW Interview" and being the most "prepared, passionate, and qualified candidate (PPQ)" are from my friend Jay Litton who develops the idea in more detail at his website www.WowInterview.com.

2. Ibid.

CHAPTER 7

1. John Piper, "30 Reasons Why It Is A Great Thing To Be a Pastor" *DesiringGod.com*. April 29, 2013. http://www.desiringgod.org/articles/30-reasons-why-it-is-a-great-thing-to-be-a-pastor.

2. Paul Vitello, "Taking a Break From the Lord's Work" *New York Times*, August 1, 2010, http://www.nytimes.com/2010/08/02/nyregion/02burnout.html.

3. "Pastors Feel Privileged and Positive, Though Discouragement Can Come" *LifeWay* Research, October 5, 2011, http://www.lifewayresearch.com/2011/10/05/pastors-feel-privileged-and-positive-though-discouragement-can-come/.

4. "Pastors' Long Work Hours Come at Expense of People, Ministry" *LifeWay* Research, January 5, 2010, http://www.lifewayresearch.com/2010/01/05/pastors-long-work-hours-come-at-expense-of-people-ministry/.

5. Ibid.

6. Eugene Cho, "Death by Ministry" http://www.churchleaders.com/pastors/pastor-articles/146201-death-by-ministry.html.

7. Thom Rainer, "Ten Trends on the Employment of Pastors." *ThomRainer.com*, April 14, 2014, http://thomrainer.com/2014/04/14/ten-trends-employment-pastors/.

CHAPTER 8

1. James M. Kouzes and Barry Posner, *The Leadership Challenge: How to Make Extraordinary Things Happen in Organizations*, (San Francisco: Jossey-Bass, 2012).

CHAPTER 9

1. This idea about vision is from Derwin L. Gray.

2. George Barna, "The Economy's Impact on Churches, Part 2 of 3," https://www.barna.org/barna-update/congregations/334-the-economys-impact-on-churches-part-2-of-3-how-churches-have-adapted#.U7r_tahZt9k.

3. "Number of Senior Workers Delaying Retirement Reaches New Post-Recession Low," *CareerBuilder.com*, February 19, 2015, http://www.careerbuilder.com/share/aboutus/pressreleasesdetail.aspx?sd=2%2F19%2F2015&id=pr869&ed=12%2F31%2F2015

4. Ibid.

5. "Correctional Populations in the United States, 2010," Bureau of Justice Statistics.

6. Matthew R. Durose, Alexia D. Cooper, and Howard N. Snyder, "Recidivism of Prisoners Released in 30 States in 2005: Patterns from 2005 to 2010," Bureau of Justice Statistics Special Report, April 2014. For more information on recidivism, visit www.nij.gov.

6. "Employment Situation Summary Table A. Household data, seasonally adjusted," Bureau of Labor Statistics, http://www.bls.gov/news.release/empsit.a.htm.

THUMBS UP

I had no idea how hard it would be to write this book.

Other things I have written – workbooks, curriculum, booklets, articles – seemed to come easily. I simply took what was in my head and put it on the page. This was different.

Perhaps it was the project size. Maybe it was the breadth and depth of the subject. Definitely it was a lack of confidence that I could do it all. Absolutely it was my misconception that I would get all the info and simply write it down.

Writing this book was a journey of discovery. It was not a single writing, but rather writing it again and again. I could not have done it alone. It took a team, or maybe better said, a community. I would like to acknowledge, that is, give thumbs up to:

Tim Krauss, my ministry partner who pushed and equipped me to do it
Justin Sabestinas, coach, editor, writing and accountability partner
Chris McGinn, writing partner, copyeditor, and encourager
Kevin Light, publishing consultant and project manager
Richard Bolles, who inspired, taught, and advised me
Pastor Derwin Gray, my pastor who supported me
Jim Buchan, advisor, equipper and encourager
Renee Swope, advisor on how to get started
Jerry Jenkins, advisor at just the right times

Now I understand why some authors say it took them all their lives to write particular books. So, therefore, I thank God for every memory of family members, friends, and servant leaders who helped save and sanctify my life.

Some are pastors:

Harry Tisdale, Holy Trinity Church
Fred Kelly, Landmark Christian Church
Tim Crater, Dunwoody Community Church
Andy Stanley and Bill Willits, North Point Community Church
Derwin L Gray and Paul Allen, Transformation Church

Most of these pastors don't know each other. They come from different denominations, backgrounds, and seminaries. Harry Tisdale has already passed on. The others are still pastoring, teaching, and preaching.

Many are leaders in ministry:

Larry Poland, Mastermedia Intl, the first ministry leader I met outside of church
Gayle Jackson and Dan Hodges, friends from church in accountability group
Bruce Wilkinson, founder of Walk Thru the Bible, teacher extraordinaire
Jimmy Collins and Truett Cathy at Chick-fil-A, ministers in business
Dr. Rick Petronella, personal counselor and friend in ministry and life
Emma Morris and Patti Gordon, friends in business, ministry, and life
Boyd Bailey, founder of Ministry Ventures, friend and mentor
Durwood Snead, friend and director of GlobalX missions
Pastor Jerry Schriver, leader Rob Snyder, and Alan Feagin
Jane Fadgen and Denny Brown, friends in launching ministry
Dave Sparkman, Bible study partner and friend in ministry
Peter Bourke, partner and friend in leading ministry
Robert and Brenda Campbell, friends and supporters for ministry and life
John Freeze, new-to-me friend, gifted, impassioned, and called to lead ministry

Three are family:

My mom and pop who gave me life and were prime examples of how to live it
My wife Kristy whom the Lord gave me to finish well keeping our eyes on Jesus

They each have breathed the life of Christ into my soul, making me a disciple, equipping me as a saint and fitting me into the body of Christ for the building up of itself in love.

Because of Jesus in them, I am still growing as a servant leader, called as a conduit to enlighten the eyes of hearts, connect people to Christ at decisive moments in their careers and equip the Church to minister to everyone in their work lives.

ABOUT THE AUTHOR

Brian Ray

Passionate about helping people find jobs, careers, and God's calling, Brian Ray founded Crossroads Career Network 15 years ago. The network grew to a national membership of churches with over 36,000 registered "career explorers and jobseekers." Brian was also the founder and owner of Primus Consulting, a retained executive search consulting firm specializing in recruiting the right people for leadership. Formerly, Brian was Vice President and Executive Committee Member of the Chick-fil-A restaurant chain, where he was responsible for Human Resources, Operator Ventures and Administration. He is the author of marketplace ministry resources: *Crossroads Career Work Book*, *Real Success at Work*, *New Job Jump Start* and *The Mastery of Leadership*. Brian and his wife Kristy are founding members of Transformation Church in Indian Land SC.

Crossroads Career
HEALTH QUIZ

WHAT IS THE CURRENT CAREER HEALTH OF YOUR CHURCH?

☐ **My church is very healthy.** Everyone is happy and fulfilled, and everyone is giving and volunteering!

☐ **My church is mostly healthy.** Most people are doing well, and we have just enough givers and volunteers to meet our church's vision.

☐ **My church is marginally healthy.** Some people are happy and fulfilled, but we have to really motivate people to give and volunteer.

☐ **My church is mostly unhealthy.** Just a few people are supporting the church with their time and money, and we have a lot of church members in job difficulty or crisis.

Take the free Crossroads Career Health Quiz - visit us online at

www.CreatedForGoodWorks.org

Get Started

Most of your church members are at a crossroads in their job or career. Ready to get started meeting the #1 need that most people want?

Take the next step and start a career ministry in your church!

Our materials are easy to use and are specifically designed to aid you in leading people to find their purpose.

We have a variety of training and ministry formats (including live, video, and online) to help you customize a plan that works for your church.

Connect with other career ministry leaders and share best practices.

Visit us online at **www.CrossroadsCareer.org**
or call **1-800-941-3566** to learn more.
Ask about special Membership options when you contact us.

Join Us in Social Media
Stay Connected on the Latest News and Events From Crossroads Career Services!

☐ Where is Brian Ray speaking?

☐ What are other churches and organizations doing in their community?

☐ What are the latest resources and tools for career ministry?

☐ What exciting new career stories are people experiencing in career ministry?

Join any of these social media networks:
Facebook.com/CrossroadsCareerNetwork
LinkedIn.com – Crossroads Career Network